Cambridge IGCSE®
Biology

Practical Workbook

Matthew Broderick

CAMBRIDGE
UNIVERSITY PRESS

CAMBRIDGE
UNIVERSITY PRESS

University Printing House, Cambridge CB2 8BS, United Kingdom

One Liberty Plaza, 20th Floor, New York, NY 10006, USA

477 Williamstown Road, Port Melbourne, VIC 3207, Australia

314–321, 3rd Floor, Plot 3, Splendor Forum, Jasola District Centre, New Delhi – 110025, India

103 Penang Road, #05-06/07, Visioncrest Commercial, Singapore 238467

Cambridge University Press is part of the University of Cambridge.

It furthers the University's mission by disseminating knowledge in the pursuit of education, learning and research at the highest international levels of excellence.

www.cambridge.org
Information on this title: www.cambridge.org/9781316611036

First published 2017

20 19 18 17 16 15 14 13 12 11 10 9 8 7 6

Printed in Great Britain by Ashford Colour Press Ltd.

A catalogue record for this publication is available from the British Library

ISBN 978-1-316-61103-6 Paperback

The questions, answers and annotation in this title were written by the author and have not been produced by Cambridge International Examinations.

The questions, answers and annotation in this title were written by the author and have not been produced by Cambridge International Examinations.

....

....

IGCSE ® is the registered trademark of Cambridge International Examinations

Contents

Introduction

Many of the great biological discoveries of our time have been made as a result of scientific investigation. From the first recorded dissection in 1275, to the first compound microscope in the 16th century, to the work of Pasteur, Pavlov, Mendel, Watson and Crick, practical biology has allowed the greatest scientific minds to measure and record their observations. These scientists followed the same scientific principles that you will follow in order to make their discoveries. It often took them years, and sometimes decades, to present their findings but do not worry, you will not have to do the same unless you are fortunate enough to work in practical biology for your career. The applications of practical biology cover much of science and could lead to careers in bioengineering, medicine, cancer research, plants and so much more. One important thing to remember is that sometimes discoveries can be serendipitous (discovered by accident, such as Tim Hunt's work on cyclins) so observe keenly and you may ascertain something that you were not even looking for.

Practical skills form the backbone of any biology course. It is hoped that, by using this book, you will gain confidence in this exciting and essential area of study. This book has been written to prepare Cambridge IGCSE biology students for both the practical paper and the alternative to practical paper. For either paper, you need to be able to demonstrate a wide range of practical skills. Through the various investigations and accompanying questions you can build and refine your abilities so that you gain enthusiasm in tackling laboratory work. Aside from the necessary exam preparation, these interesting and enjoyable investigations are intended to kindle a passion for practical biology. Great care has been taken to ensure that this book contains work that is safe and accessible for you to complete. Before attempting any of these activities, though, make sure that you have read the safety section and are following the safety regulations of the place where you study.

Answers to the exercises in this Workbook can be found in the Teacher's guide. Ask your teacher to provide access to the answers.

Safety section

Despite using Bunsen burners and chemicals on a regular basis, the science laboratory is one of the safest classrooms in a school. This is due to the emphasis on safety and the following of precautions set out by regular risk assessment and procedures.

It is imperative that you follow the safety rules set out by your teacher. Your teacher will know the names of materials and the hazards associated with them as part of their risk assessment for performing the investigations. They will share this information with you as part of their safety brief or demonstration of the investigation.

The safety precautions in each of the investigations of this book are guidance that you should follow. You should aim to use the safety rules as further direction to help to prepare for examination when planning your own investigations in the alternative to practical papers.

The following precautions will help to ensure your safety when carrying out most investigations in this workbook.

- Wear safety spectacles to protect your eyes.
- Tie back hair and any loose items of clothing.
- Personal belongings should be tidied away to avoid tripping over them.
- Wear gloves and protective clothing as described in the book or by your teacher.
- Turn the Bunsen burner to the cool, yellow flame when not in use.
- Observe hazard symbols and chemical information provided with all substances and solutions.

Many of the investigations require some sort of teamwork or group work. It is the responsibility of your group to make sure that you plan how to be safe as diligently as you plan the rest of the investigation.

Skills grid

Assessment objective 3 (AO3) 'Experimental skills and investigations' of the Cambridge International Examinations syllabus is about your ability to work as a scientist. Each aspect of the AO3 has been broken down for you below with a reference to the chapters in this title that cover it. This will enable you to identify where you have practiced each skill and also allow you to revise each one before the exam.

Chapter	1	2	3	4	5	6	7	8	9	10	11	12	13	14	15	16	17	18	19	20	21	22
A03: Experimental skills and investigations																						
1.1 demonstrate knowledge of how to safely use techniques	X	X	X	X	X	X	X	X	X	X	X	X	X	X	X	X	X	X	X	X	X	X
1.2 demonstrate knowledge of how to use apparatus and materials	X	X	X	X	X	X	X	X	X	X	X	X	X	X	X	X	X	X	X	X	X	X
1.3 demonstrate knowledge of how to follow a sequence of instructions where appropriate	X	X	X	X	X	X	X	X	X	X	X	X	X	X	X	X	X	X	X	X	X	X
2 plan experiments and investigations		X	X	X		X	X	X	X	X	X				X	X					X	
3.1 make and record observations	X	X	X	X	X	X	X	X	X	X	X	X	X	X	X	X	X	X	X	X	X	X
3.2 make and record measurements	X	X	X		X	X	X	X	X	X	X	X	X	X	X			X	X	X	X	X
3.3 make and record estimates		X				X			X	X			X		X	X		X	X	X	X	X
4.1 interpret experimental observations and data	X	X	X	X	X	X	X	X	X	X	X	X	X	X	X	X	X	X	X	X	X	X
4.2 evaluate experimental observations and data			X	X	X	X	X		X	X			X	X	X	X			X	X	X	X
5.1 evaluate methods		X	X	X	X	X	X	X	X	X	X	X	X	X	X	X	X	X	X	X	X	X
5.2 suggest possible improvements to methods		X	X		X		X		X		X	X	X	X	X				X		X	X
Additional non-A03 skills for biology																						
Biological drawings or sketches	X	X	X	X		X	X	X	X	X	X	X			X	X			X		X	
Constructing own table			X	X	X		X	X	X		X		X	X	X	X			X	X	X	
Drawing/analysing a graph					X	X		X	X		X			X					X	X	X	
Planning safety of an investigation		X	X	X		X	X		X	X		X			X						X	
Mathematical calculations		X			X		X	X			X	X	X	X	X	X			X		X	

Quick skills section

Apparatus

You will need to be able to identify, use and draw a variety of scientific apparatus. Complete the table below by adding a diagram and uses for each piece of apparatus.

Apparatus	Diagram	Uses
timer		
balance/scales		
beaker		
pipette		

burette		
conical flask		
Bunsen burner		
tripod		
test-tube / boiling tube		

Measuring

Being able to take **accurate** measurements is an essential skill for all biology students. As part of the Cambridge IGCSE course you will be expected to be able to take accurate measurements using a variety of different apparatus. When using measuring cylinders, you will need to look for the **meniscus**, which is the bottom of the curve formed by the liquid.

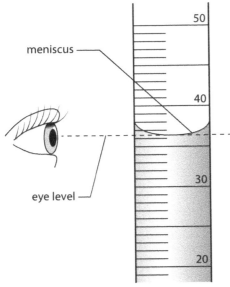

Thermometers are a very common tool for measuring temperature in biology experiments so you will need to be able to take **reliable** readings. Not all of the points on the scale on a thermometer will be marked but you will still need to be able to determine the temperature. To do this you will need to work out the value of each graduation. In the diagram below there are four marks between 95 and 100. Each of these marks indicates 1 °C.

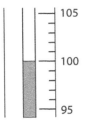

Biological drawings

It is important that you can draw what you see when observing biological specimens, whether this is under a microscope, using a magnifying glass, or observing with your eyes only. You are not expected to be an accomplished artist but your drawing should convey what you see as clearly as possible. Your drawings, sketches and diagrams should meet the following **expectations**:

- Drawn using a sharp pencil
- Draw clear, unbroken lines
- Avoid shading or colouring unless stated otherwise
- Drawn to scale unless stated otherwise
- Drawn as large, or larger, than the specimen unless stated otherwise
- Major structures or features should be clearly labelled using a ruler

Recording

When working on investigations, the ability to record data accurately is very important. Sometimes a table will be supplied; however, you need to be able to draw your own table with the correct headings and units. The first task is to identify the independent and dependent variables for the investigation you are doing.

- The **independent variable** is the one which you are changing to see if this affects the dependent variable.
- The **dependent variable** is the one which you will measure and record the results of in the table.

The variables and their units need to go into the top two boxes in your results table. The independent variable goes in the left-hand box and the dependent variable goes in the right-hand box. Separate the name of the variables and units using a forward slash /, e.g. time / seconds. Remember that the column headings need to be physical quantities (time, mass, temperature. etc.)

Next, count how many different values you have for the independent variable. This is how many rows you will need to add below the column headings. Finally, add the values for the independent variable into the left-hand column. Your table is now ready for you to add the results from your investigation in the right-hand column.

Independent variable / units	Dependent variable / units

Graphing

The type of graph you opt to draw is likely to depend on the type of data you are recording:

- Pie charts: These should be drawn with the sectors in rank order, largest first, beginning at 'noon' and proceeding clockwise. Pie charts should preferably contain no more than six sectors.
- Bar charts: These should be drawn when one of the variables is not numerical. They should be made up of narrow blocks of equal width that do **not** touch.
- Histograms: These should be drawn when plotting frequency graphs with continuous data. The blocks should be drawn in order of increasing or decreasing magnitude and they **should** touch.

Whichever type of graph you draw however, it is useful you follow a set procedure every time to ensure that, when you are finished, the graph is complete.

Axes – You must label the axes with your independent and dependent variables. The independent variable is used to label the x-axis (horizontal axis) and the dependent variable is used to label the y-axis (vertical axis). Remember to also add the units for each of the variables. An easy way to ensure that you get this correct is to copy the column headings from the table of data you are using to draw the graph.

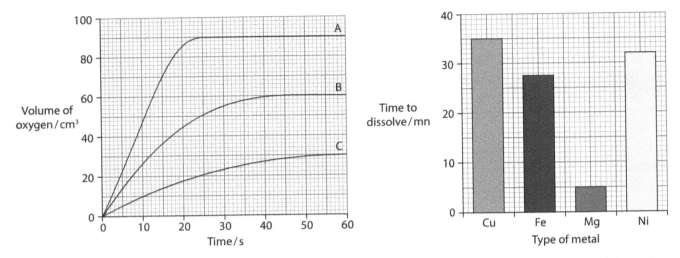

Tip – At the top of any table of data you have to use, write the letters X and Y next to the independent and dependent variable to remind you which axis each goes on.

The second stage of drawing a graph is adding a **scale**. You must select a scale that allows you to use more than half of the graph grid in both directions. Choose a sensible ratio to allow you to easily plot your points (e.g. each 1 cm on the graph grid represents 1, 2, 5, 10, 50 or 100 units of the variable). If you choose to use other numbers for your scale, it becomes much more difficult to plot your graph. This skill gets easier the more times you draw a graph. If you have done this lightly with a pencil, you can easily make adjustments until you are fully skilled.

Now you are ready to plot the **points** of data on the graph grid. You can use either crosses (×) or a point enclosed inside a circle to plot your points but take your time to make sure these are plotted accurately. Remember to use a sharp pencil as large dots make it difficult to see the place the point is plotted and may make it difficult for the accuracy of the plot to be decided.

Finally, a **best-fit line** needs to be added. This must be a single thin line or smooth curve. It does not need to go through all of the points but it should have roughly half the number of points on each side of the data scattered. Remember to ignore any anomalous data when you draw your best-fit line. Some good examples of best-fit lines are shown below:

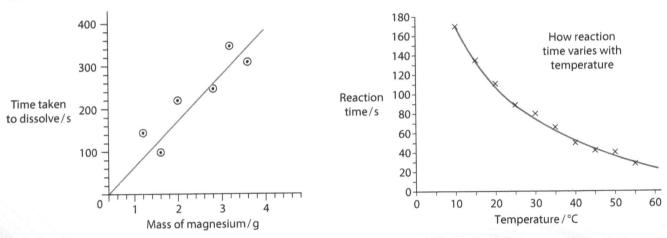

Variables

The independent and dependent variables have already been discussed but there is a third type of variable that you will need to be familiar with – **controlled variables**. These are variables that are kept the same during an investigation to make sure that they do not affect the results. If these variables are not kept the same, then we cannot be sure that it is our independent variable having an effect on the results. The more variables that you can control, the more reliable your investigation will be.

Example

Two students are investigating how changing the temperature affects the rate at which starch is broken down by amylase. They do not control the quantity of amylase or starch used each time. This means that there is no pattern in their results because, if they use more starch and amylase, the amount of glucose produced will be increased regardless of the temperatures used.

Reliability, accuracy and precision

A common task in this book will be to suggest how to improve the method used in an investigation to improve its reliability/accuracy/precision. Before we come to how these improvements can be made it is important that you have an understanding of what each of these words means.

Reliability is about the likelihood of getting the same results if you did the investigation again and being sure that the results are not just down to chance. Reliability is now often called repeatability for this reason. If you can repeat an investigation several times and get the same result each time, it is said to be reliable.

Improve the reliability of your investigation by:
- controlling other variables well so they do not affect the results
- repeating the experiment until no anomalous results are achieved.

Precision
Precise results have very little deviance from the mean.

Improve the precision of your investigation by:
- using apparatus that has smaller scale divisions.

Accuracy is a measure of how close the measured value is to the true value. The accuracy of the results depends on the measuring apparatus used and the skill of the person taking the measurements.

Improve the accuracy of your results by:
- improving the design of an investigation to reduce errors
- using more precise apparatus
- repeating the measurement and calculating the mean.

You can observe how these terms are used in the following figure.

Reliability v Precision v Accuracy

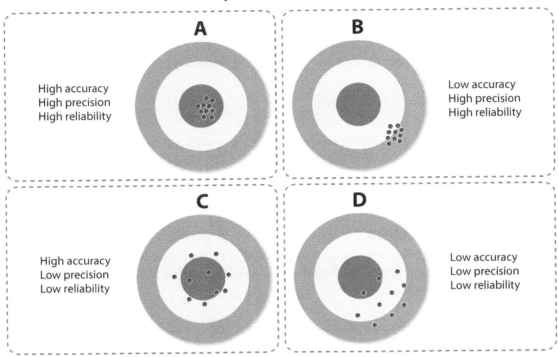

A

High accuracy
High precision
High reliability

B

Low accuracy
High precision
High reliability

C

High accuracy
Low precision
Low reliability

D

Low accuracy
Low precision
Low reliability

Validity

Validity is the confidence that scientists put into a set of results and the conclusions that they draw from them. Results are considered valid if they measure what they were designed to, and if they are precise, accurate and reliable.

Designing an investigation

When asked to design an investigation, you must think carefully about what level of detail to include. The following is an example of how to create a method. Follow these steps to be able to design reliable, accurate investigations.

1   Identify what your independent variable is and the range of values that you are planning to use for it.
2   The dependent variable must also be identified along with how (using equipment and apparatus) you are going to measure it.
3   Suggest how you will control other variables.
4   Outline the method in a series of numbered steps that is detailed enough for someone else to follow.
5   Remember to include repeat readings to help improve reliability.
6   Check the validity of your investigation and results.
7   You must also include any hazards and safety warnings, as well as safety equipment that should be used in the investigation.

1 Classification

Overview

In this chapter, you will review the main characteristics of different organisms and identify different groups of organisms using their features. You should also be able to identify the key features of a living organism in a living thing.

Practical investigation 1.1 Drawing and labelling organisms

Objective

The aim is to collect samples of different organisms to draw and label in the classroom. You should consider the key characteristics of life (using the acronym MRSGREN) to confirm whether your chosen specimen is a living organism or not. You should also begin to develop the required skills to draw and label what you can see accurately.

Equipment

- Small tray or box
- Latex gloves
- Insect pooter (optional)
- Sharp pencil
- Forceps/tweezers (or small shovel)

Method

1   You will need to gather the equipment provided by your teacher (this may or may not include an insect pooter).
2   Using the time and area allocated, search the area for organisms that can be collected in your tray. You should use gloves and forceps to protect your hands.
3   Collect at least three items that you consider to be organisms and place them in the tray or collect them by using the insect pooter.
4   Take your samples back to the classroom for drawing and observation.
5   Make large drawings of three of your samples in the boxes in the 'Recording data' section. Use the table in 'Analysis' to help guide your drawings. Label as many obvious or distinguishing features as you can see.
6   Once you have finished, you should safely dispose of any organisms that you collected. Your teacher will advise you on the disposal method. All live animals should be returned to the habitat where you found them.

Safety considerations

- Wear gloves and use forceps/tweezers when handling organisms.
- Wash your hands afterwards.
- Your teacher will give you any further safety instructions that are relevant to your local environment, such as dangerous insects or plants that can harm you.

Recording data

1   Make large labelled drawings of three samples and complete the information next to each box.

Name of organism ....

Location found ....

Observable signs that the sample is a living organism

....

....

Handling data

2 For any one of your drawings, use a ruler to measure the length of the actual organism and the length of your drawing of that organism. Use this information to calculate the magnification of your drawing.

Magnification: ....

Analysis

3 You should select one of your drawings for the analysis of your drawing skills. Complete the table to check the quality of your drawing. Then, swap with one of your classmates and allow them to mark your efforts.

Drawing skill	Self-graded	Graded by a classmate
Used a sharp pencil		
Drawn smooth, single lines		
The specimen is the right shape and proportion		
The drawing is larger than the actual specimen		
All observable features are drawn		
Labelled lines are neat and drawn with a ruler, touching the feature		
You have not used shading or colours in your diagram		
Total marks (out of 7)		

Evaluation

4 Look at the table in the 'Analysis' section. Do you have full marks from yourself and your peer? If not, identify the areas where you could improve and write them in the space below. You will need to refer to this next time you make a biological drawing of a specimen.

- ....
- ....
- ....
- ....

5 Complete the following table with the missing characteristics of life, then show which of the characteristics, if any, were evident in your collected specimens.

Characteristics of life	Specimen	Evidence that I could see
movement		
respiration		
growth		
excretion		
nutrition		

Practical investigation 1.2 Observation and drawing of pollen tubes

Objective

The aim of this investigation is to dissect a flower, make a detailed drawing of the inside of the flower, label the features, and identify the different sections within the flower. This builds upon the drawing skills developed in Practical investigation 1.1 and link to knowledge of the plant group that your flower falls into (such as angiosperm/monocot/dicot).

Equipment

- Scalpel
- Dissection tray or board
- Different types of flower

Method

1   Set up the dissection area on your workbench.
2   Carefully cut your flower into half to create a cross-section of the inside of the flower. You are aiming to observe the pollen tubes.
3   Repeat this to allow each member of the group to have their cross-section of the flower for drawing.
4   Make a large, detailed drawing of your cross-section of the flower.

Safety considerations

Take care when using the scalpel. Clear stains using paper towels if they spill onto the workbench.

Recording data

Make your large, detailed drawing in the box below and label the parts that you know.

Name of flower ....

Class of the flower ....

Analysis

1 In the previous investigation, you assessed your biological drawing using the criteria in the table. This time, you should list the criteria below that your diagram meets from that list.

- ....
- ....
- ....
- ....
- ....
- ....
- ....

Evaluation

2 Now, refer back to the list and write down the criteria, if any, that you did not meet in your flower drawing.

- ....
- ....
- ....

3 What class of plant does your flower belong to?

....

Exam-style question

1 The yellow-fever mosquito (*Aedes aegypti*) is found in many tropical regions around the world and is identifiable by white markings on its legs. (Figure 1.1)

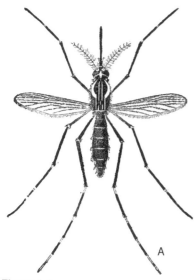

A

Figure 1.1

a Make a large drawing of the mosquito in the space below. [5]

b What is the actual size of the leg marked 'A' on the mosquito? [1]

....

c What is the size of the same leg in your own drawing? [1]

....

d Use your previous answers to calculate the magnification of your drawing. [3]

....

e Which genus does the yellow-fever mosquito belong to? [1]

....

f Which group of organisms does the yellow-fever mosquito belong to? [1]

....

Total [12]

2 Cells

Overview

In this chapter, you will review the different structures and organelles that make up different cells in the plant and animal kingdoms. You will observe the similarities and differences between the levels of organisation and be able to recognise these using a light microscope. You will also learn how to calculate the size of specimens and have further opportunities to practise the skill of producing a biological drawing of a specimen learnt in Chapter 1.

Practical investigation 2.1 Observing plant cells

Objective

This investigation aims to develop your basic microscope skills in order to safely observe plant cells using a light microscope. You will observe some of the different structures in these cells and relate them to their functions.

Equipment

- Light microscope
- Microscope slide
- Cover slip
- Forceps

- Scalpel
- Safety spectacles
- Staining solution
  (1% methylene blue or iodine)

- Sample of onion (or similar)
- Mounted needle
- Filter paper or paper towel

Method

1 Set up your microscope safely as shown by your teacher.
2 Remove a small piece of the single, inner layer of onion cells (the epidermis) using a scalpel and forceps.
3 Place the layer of epithelial cells onto the microscope slide with no folds.
4 Add a drop of the staining solution to the onion sample. Excess solution can be removed by using filter paper or a paper towel.
5 Place the cover slip onto the sample by lowering at an angle with a mounted needle (or similar) as shown in Figure 2.1.
6 Tap the cover slip lightly with the end of a pencil.
7 Place the specimen onto the microscope stage.
8 Allow light to shine onto the specimen and begin at the lowest magnification.
9 Slowly turn the focusing wheel until you begin to see your specimen.
10 Use the fine focusing wheel to sharpen the image.
11 Sketch a diagram of what you can see through the lens.
12 Repeat using different magnifications – move upwards through the different magnifications of your microscope to see more detail at each level.

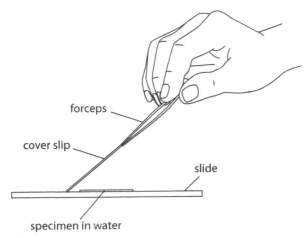

forceps

cover slip

slide

specimen in water

Figure 2.1

Safety considerations

- Wear safety spectacles (and gloves if available) as some staining solutions are irritants.
- Take care when using a scalpel and store it safely when not in use.
- Report broken glass to the teacher.
- Take care with coarse adjustments on the microscope to avoid breaking slides.
- Beware of the lens becoming very hot when using a microscope.

Recording data

1   Sketch a diagram of what you observe through the microscope lens in the space below. You may choose to draw more than one cell, as there may be many hundred cells in your field of view. You should label your diagram and use the drawing skills learnt in Chapter 1 to guide you.

Magnification: ....

Magnification: ....

Handling data

2   What was the total magnification for the specimen that you drew?
Remember the equation: Total magnification = magnification of objective lens × magnification of eyepiece lens
Total magnification = ...

Analysis

3   State the structures of the plant cell that you observed through your light microscope.

....

....

....

4 State the structures of an onion cell that you cannot see using a light microscope.

....

....

....

Evaluation

5 Why was it important to use only a single layer of onion cells for your specimen?

....

6 What was the purpose of staining the plant cells?

....

Practical investigation 2.2 Observing animal cells

Objective

To use the microscope skills developed during Practical investigation 2.1 to prepare and observe human cheek cells. The structure of cheek cells makes them more difficult to see under a light microscope but you will see them at different magnifications in this investigation.

Equipment

- Light microscope
- Cotton bud
- Disinfectant solution
- Safety spectacles
- Disposable gloves
- Staining solution (iodine or methylene blue)
- Microscope slide
- Cover slip
- Mounted needle

Method

1   Your teacher will demonstrate how to take a sample of human cheek cells. You should use this demonstration and your knowledge from the previous investigation to plan a method in the space below. Take care to observe the subtle differences in preparing this slide.

....

....

....

....

....

....

....

....

Safety considerations

- Place cotton buds into the disinfectant solution immediately after use.
- Wear safety spectacles and gloves at all times.
- Report broken glass to the teacher immediately.
- Take care when using a light microscope as the lens can become very hot.

Recording data

2   State five different criteria that should be met when drawing a biological specimen.

....

....

....

....

....

3 Sketch a diagram of what you observe through the microscope lens in the space below, at two different magnifications. You should label your diagrams and state the magnification used on both occasions.

Magnification: ....   Magnification: ....

Analysis

4 Complete the following table by ticking the boxes to show which organelles are visible when using a light microscope.

Organelle	Onion cell	Human cheek cell	Function
nucleus			
cell wall			
cell membrane			
cytoplasm			
ribosomes			
chloroplasts			

5 Give the name of the organelle that is the site of aerobic respiration.

....

Evaluation

6 How could you view parts of organelles that were not visible using a light microscope?

....

....

7 Explain why the cotton buds were placed into disinfectant or sterilising fluid after being used to collect the cell sample.

....

Practical investigation 2.3 Drawing different specimens

Objective

In this investigation, you will observe some microscope slide preparations of specialised cells and tissues from different organisms to further develop your microscope skills. Some of the samples may have complicated structures which will allow you to practise your drawing skills, and some samples will have very small cells that require you to demonstrate, and develop, your microscope skills.

Equipment

- Light microscope
- Pre-mounted slides of different cells and tissues

Method

1   Set up your microscope carefully and safely like you have done in the previous investigations.
2   View the different slides available under your microscope. View your specimen using the different magnifications to find the clearest view of the specimen.
3   Draw and label the different cells and tissues that you observe. It may be that you only find one or two cells and can draw them. If you have a large number of cells or tissue, you can draw a section of what you can see in your field of view.
4   Working in pairs, take turns to find a specimen and explain to each other what you can see and how the structure of that cell/tissue allows it to carry out its function.

Safety considerations

Notify your teacher of any broken glass.

Recording data

1   Make labelled drawings of what you see in the spaces below. Include a description of what you were looking at and the magnification of the microscope. This is the third time that you have done this; it is expected that you are meeting all of the minimum criteria of a good biological drawing.

Magnification: ....   Magnification: ....

Magnification: ....

Magnification: ....

Analysis

2 Define the term **tissue**, giving one example from the slides that you viewed.

....

....

3 Name the organ that your answer to Question 2 might be found in.

....

Evaluation

4 This exercise requires excellent focusing skills when using the microscope to view your specimen as clearly as possible. Describe how you used the microscope to achieve this, naming the different parts that are required.

....

....

....

....

Practical investigation 2.4 Measuring and calculating the size of specimens

Objective

In this investigation, you will use the following formula to calculate the real size of the cells or tissue that you view under the microscope:

$$\text{Magnification} = \frac{\text{image size of specimen}}{\text{actual size of specimen}}$$

You will measure specimens using millimetres (mm) and micrometres (μm) as standard units. You will demonstrate the ability to plan an investigation independently that will allow you to observe human cheek cells under the microscope.

Equipment

1   Complete the list of equipment required to observe a sample of your cheek cells.

- Light microscope
- ....
- ....
- ....
- ....
- ....
- ....
- ....
- ....

Method

2   Plan a suitable method for obtaining, and observing, a sample of your cheek cells.

1   ....

2   ....

3   ....

4   ....

5   ....

6   ....

7   ....

8   ....

Safety considerations

3 Note down the safety precautions you should take for this investigation.

....

....

....

....

Recording data

4 In the space provided below, make a labelled drawing of what you see. Include a description of what you are looking at and the magnification of the microscope. You should aim for this exercise to see at least one cheek cell at the highest magnification possible.

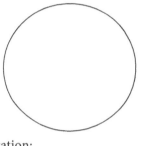

Magnification: ....

Analysis and handling data

5 Once you have found your image, you will be able to calculate the actual size of the cells in view by using this method:

a Place a clear plastic ruler on the stage with one of the scale marks on the edge of the field of view.

b Count the number of millimetre (mm) spaces in the field of view to measure the size of the field of view

Size of field of view ....mm

c Convert this to micrometres (μm) by multiplying by 1000

Size of field of view ....μm

d Estimate the number of cells across your field of view. (In other words, how many of your cheek cells would cross from one side to the other in a straight line?)

Number of cells across the field of view ....

e You can then use the following formula:

$$\text{Length of one cell} = \frac{\text{diameter of field of view}}{\text{estimated number of cells across the field of view}}$$

Length of one cell = ... μm

For example, if the diameter of the field of view is 4.2 mm (or 4200 μm) and you estimate that 24 cells would cross the diameter from end to end, then 4.2 mm ÷ 24 cells = 0.175 mm (or 175 μm)

Evaluation

6 Explain why calculating the size of onion cells is easier than calculating the size of cheek cells. Think about how the onion cells would have been arranged in your field of view.

....

....

....

7 Onion epidermal cells do not contain chloroplasts. Give the name of one plant cell that does contain a large number of chloroplasts.

....

Exam-style questions

1 Look at the invertebrate shown in Figure 2.2.

Figure 2.2

a Make a large, detailed drawing of this animal. [5]

b Measure the length of the animal in Figure 2.2. .... [1]

c Measure the length of the same animal in your drawing. .... [1]

d Calculate the magnification of your drawing.

Magnification of drawing = ... [3]

Total [10]

2 Heather is preparing a sample of human cheek cells on a microscope slide. She uses a 1% methylene blue solution to stain the cells and views the cells at a magnification of ×400.

a What safety precautions should Heather take when preparing and viewing her cheek cells? [3]

....

....

....

b Which organelles should Heather expect to see at ×400 under a light microscope? [2]

....

....

....

c Heather calculates that the image size of her cheek cell is 0.2 mm. What is the actual size of one of Heather's cheek cells? [2]

....

....

....

Total [7]

3 Movement in and out of cells

Overview

In this chapter, you will observe the processes of diffusion and osmosis. This provides you with the opportunity to test the predictions that you make about how some substances will behave when placed in different solutions.

Practical investigation 3.1 Diffusion in gelatine products

Objective

The objective of this investigation is to observe diffusion in action. This requires some chemistry knowledge as you will be using gelatine. Gelatine contains a chemical that is an excellent indicator of pH because the chemical is red in alkaline conditions but turns yellow under acidic conditions. You will test your observation skills here and you will be expected to link what is happening to your knowledge of diffusion to explain what happens.

Equipment

- Red gelatine/jelly
- Scalpel or knife
- ($1 \, mol \, dm^{-3}$) hydrochloric acid
- Test-tube and bung
- Safety spectacles

Method

1   Cut a piece of gelatine that will fit inside a test-tube.
2   Add the hydrochloric acid to cover the gelatine.
3   Place the bung firmly into the top of the test-tube.
4   Place the test-tube horizontally (making sure it cannot roll off the table).
5   Observe what happens to the colour of the gelatine.

Safety considerations

- Take care when using the scalpel.
- Wear safety spectacles when handling hydrochloric acid.

Recording data

1   Write down what happened to the block of red gelatine.

....

....

Analysis

2 Using your knowledge of diffusion, explain what happened to cause the change in colour that you observed. You should aim to use the following words in your explanation.

> diffusion   higher concentration   acidic   movement

....

....

....

Evaluation

3 You decide to repeat this experiment three times to check your results. What steps would you take to ensure that you carry out a reliable test?

....

....

....

Practical investigation 3.2 Osmosis in potatoes

Objective

The objective of this investigation is to gather reliable data and use this to support knowledge about the process of osmosis. You will control the variables of the investigation to ensure its validity. This investigation will provide you with a real example of osmosis taking place to support your understanding.

Equipment

- Potato
- Cork borer
- Clear plastic ruler
- Distilled water
- 30% sucrose solution

- 70% sucrose solution
- Test-tubes ×6 and rack
- Scalpel or knife
- Pen/marker for writing on test tubes

- Safety spectacles
- Measuring cylinder
- Paper towel

Method

1 Use the cork borer to bore out six cylinders of potato tissue of similar length.
2 Use the ruler and scalpel to cut the cylinders of potato tissue to exactly the same length.
3 Record this length in the table in the 'Recording data' section.
4 Pour the same amount of distilled water into two of the test-tubes and mark them for identification.
5 Pour the same amount of 30% sucrose solution into two of the test-tubes and mark them.
6 Pour the same amount of 70% sucrose solution into two of the test-tubes and mark them.
7 Add the potato sections at the same time and leave for 15 minutes.
8 After 15 minutes, remove the potato tissue samples from the solutions and pat dry using a paper towel.
9 Measure the length of each potato tissue sample and record the details in the table.

Safety considerations

- Take care when using the borer and the scalpel.
- Wear safety spectacles at all times.

Recording data

1 Complete the table and record your results. Make sure that you add the units to your table headings and the types of solution that you used in this investigation.

Solution	Length of potato tissue sample before treatment /......................			Length of potato tissue sample after treatment /......................			Average change in length /......................
	Sample 1	Sample 2	Average	Sample 1	Sample 2	Average	
distilled water							

2 Look closely at the appearance of the potato tissue samples. Describe the differences between the tissue samples that were in the different solutions. Use keywords such as turgid and flaccid as part of your answer.

....

....

....

Handling data

3 Describe how you calculated the average length of each of the potato tissue samples.

....

....

....

Analysis

4 Describe and explain the results that you observed in your investigation. Use the data from your completed table to support your answer.

....

....

....

....

....

....

Evaluation

5 State what you did in this investigation to make your results more valid.

....

....

....

....

6 Identify the possible source of error in step 4 of the method and make a suggestion for improvement.

....

....

....

Practical investigation 3.3 Osmotic turgor

Objective

In this investigation, you will investigate osmotic turgor using Visking tubing and relate this to your knowledge of diffusion and osmosis.

Equipment

- Safety spectacles
- Test-tube and rack
- Syrup solution
- 20 cm Visking tubing
- Distilled water
- Elastic band
- Graduated pipette

Method

1   The Visking tubing has been soaked in water in advance for you. Tie a tight knot in one end of the tubing.
2   Add 4 cm³ of the syrup solution to the other end of the tubing and tightly knot that end.
3   Wash the outside of the tubing in cold water.
4   Do not overfill your piece of tubing. Ensure that you can bend it in half.
5   Place the tubing inside the test-tube (you can secure this by using an elastic band to secure the excess tubing after the knot).
6   Fill the test-tube with water and leave for 30 minutes.

Safety considerations

Wear safety spectacles throughout the investigation.

Recording data

1   Sketch a diagram of the Visking tubing before and after your investigation to illustrate how it changed.

before

after

Analysis

2 Describe the difference between the test two tubes before and after the investigation.

....

....

3 Explain why the tubing changed during the investigation.

....

....

Evaluation

4 Suggest what might have happened if the tubing had been left inside the test-tube for an extra hour.

....

....

5 Why was the tubing washed with cold water in Step 3 of the method?

....

....

Practical investigation 3.4 Planning an investigation into osmosis

Objective

In this investigation, you will plan your own investigation on osmosis using skills from the rest of the chapter. You will evaluate your investigation and suggest improvements in reliability.

Your task is to plan each stage of the investigation independently using the materials provided.

Equipment

- Potato
- Cork borer
- Balance/weighing scales
- Safety spectacles
- Stopwatch
- Marker pen
- Distilled water
- 20% sugar solution
- Test-tubes × 4 and rack

Method

1   Plan your method here, using only the equipment from the list above.

    ....
    ....
    ....
    ....
    ....
    ....
    ....
    ....

Safety considerations

2   Suggest at least two safety measures that should be taken in this investigation.

    ....
    ....
    ....

Recording data

3 Draw and complete a table to record your results of the investigation. Hint: the independent variable should be in the left-hand column of the table and you should include the units in the headings of the table.

Handling data

4 Use this space to calculate the percentage change in the mass of the potato tissue samples in your investigation.

Analysis

5 Describe and explain what happened in your investigation.

....

....

....

....

Evaluation

6 Suggest one way that you could improve the reliability of the data collected in the investigation.

....

....

Exam-style questions

1 Starch solution was placed inside a piece of Visking tubing which was submerged inside a test-tube of iodine solution, as shown in Figure 3.1. After 15 minutes, the contents were observed.

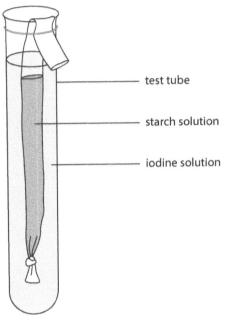

— test tube

— starch solution

— iodine solution

Figure 3.1

a Describe the colour change, if any, which takes place inside the Visking tubing. [2]

....

....

b Explain why the colour change did not occur in both solutions. [2]

....

....

....

c Describe the safety precautions that should be taken for this investigation. [2]

....

....

Total [6]

2 Shelton cuts nine pieces of potato and measures their mass. He places three pieces of potato into three different solutions and leaves them for 1 hour. The pieces of potato were removed and their masses were measured again. The table shows Shelton's results for the investigation.

| Solution | Mass of potato tissue sample / .... | | |
	Before	After	Change
distilled water	1.69	1.83	
	1.52	1.78	
	1.57	1.70	
20% sucrose solution	1.51	1.40	
	1.91	1.65	
	1.69	1.30	
40% sucrose solution	1.54	1.01	
	1.60	1.12	
	1.77	1.18	

a Complete the table to show the change in mass for each of the potato tissue samples. [4]

b Calculate the mean change in mass of the potato tissue samples in each of the different solutions. [3]

Distilled water: .... g

20% sucrose solution .... g

40% sucrose solution .... g

c Describe and explain the mean mass change of the potato tissue samples in each of the different solutions. [4]

....

....

....

....

....

....

d Suggest why Shelton used three pieces of potato in each of the different solutions during his investigation. [1]

....

....

Total [12]

4 The chemicals of life

Overview

In this chapter, you will investigate how to test for the presence of carbohydrates, protein and fats in foodstuffs. This will support your knowledge of the smaller molecules that make up larger molecules, such as starch and proteins. You will also extract DNA from a sample of your own saliva.

Practical investigation 4.1 Testing for the presence of carbohydrates

Objective

You will investigate how to test for reducing sugars and starch. You will describe these tests and understand how they can be used in the analysis of foodstuffs.

Equipment

- Test-tubes × 5
- 20% glucose solution
- Vegetable oil
- Safety spectacles
- Water

- Test-tube rack
- Alcohol
- Pipettes
- Hot water (water bath)
- 1% starch solution

- 1% protein solution
- Biuret solution
- Iodine solution
- Benedict's solution

Method

1   Prepare three of the test-tubes with approximately 20 ml (or the width of two fingers) of each of the following solutions: starch solution (test-tube A), protein solution (test-tube B), glucose solution (test-tube C).
2   Add the following to each of the test-tubes and record your observations in a table in the 'Recording data' section.
    a   Add three drops of iodine solution to test-tube A.
    b   Add three drops of biuret solution to test-tube B.
    c   Add three drops of Benedict's solution to test-tube C. Place test-tube C into a beaker of hot/boiling water for 5 minutes before observing.
3   Add 5 ml of alcohol to test-tube D followed by two drops of vegetable oil. Shake gently to dissolve the fat.
4   Add 3 ml of water to test-tube E. Pour the contents of test-tube D into test-tube E and record your observations.

Safety considerations

- Wear safety spectacles at all times.
- Do not ingest or inhale any of the solutions.
- Report all spillages and breakages to the teacher.

Recording data

1 Draw a table to record your observations. You should name the solutions used and note your observations. Make sure you have enough space for a small diagram to sketch what happened in each case.

Handling data

For each of the solutions tested, state the positive result for the following:

2 Starch solution tested with iodine:

....

3 Protein solution tested with biuret test:

....

4 Glucose solution (reducing sugar) tested with Benedict's solution:

....

5 Vegetable oil tested with a mixture of alcohol and water:

....

Practical investigation 4.2 Extracting DNA

Objective

This investigation is aimed at giving you the opportunity to follow a method to safely extract your own DNA. You can then observe the precipitated DNA and relate this to your knowledge of its structure.

Equipment

- Drinking water
- Salt
- Clear drinking cups
- Washing-up liquid
- Food colouring
- Glass beaker × 2
- Glass rods
- 100 ml isopropyl alcohol
- Safety spectacles

Method

1   Mix the drinking water with some salt in a beaker. Stir until all of the salt has dissolved.
2   Transfer approximately 50 ml of the salt water into the drinking cup.
3   Gargle all of the water for 60 seconds.
4   Spit the water back into a glass beaker.
5   Add a small drop of washing-up liquid to the salt water.
6   Use the glass rod to stir gently without creating any air bubbles.
7   Add 3 drops of food colouring to the alcohol in a clean cup.
8   Tilt the saltwater cup at about 45° and gently pour the alcohol/food colouring mix into the saltwater cup. The alcohol mixture should trickle slowly down the side to reach the salt water mix as slowly as possible.
9   The alcohol mixture will form a layer on top of the salt water if you pour slowly enough.
10 Leave the solution for 3 minutes and observe.
11 The white clumps and string that form are your DNA!

Safety considerations

- Wear safety spectacles.
- Take care when using alcohol and do not ingest.

Analysis

1   Describe the shape of the precipitated DNA that you can see in your suspension.

....

....

....

Evaluation

2   Did everyone in the class achieve an extraction of DNA? If not, why do you think this might have been?

....

....

....

Practical investigation 4.3 Testing foods

Objective

In this investigation, you will apply your knowledge from Practical investigation 4.1 to test different foodstuffs and find out what macronutrients they contain. Your ability to plan and select the appropriate method will be tested here, as well as your observational skills.

Equipment

- Test-tubes and/or spotting tiles
- Safety spectacles
- Water
- Test-tube rack

- Alcohol
- Pipettes
- Range of food and drink
- Pestle and mortar

- Hot water (water bath)
- Biuret solution
- Iodine solution
- Benedict's solution

Method

1   Select three different types of food or drink substances from the selection available and devise a suitable test to determine if they contain reducing sugars, protein, starch or fat. In the following spaces, plan a method to carry out the tests.

    Test 1

    Test 2

    Test 3

Safety considerations

2 State two safety requirements that you will need to follow for this investigation.

....

....

Recording data

3 Complete the table to show the results of your tests. Tick the test that you carried out.

Food/Drink	Test for reducing sugar	Test for protein	Test for fat	Test for starch

Analysis

4 For each of the foodstuffs that you tested, describe what you observed and state the macronutrients that each food contained.

....

....

....

....

....

....

Evaluation

5 How could your investigation be improved or the results be made more reliable?

....

....

Exam-style questions

1   Moira carries out an investigation on reducing sugars. She tests three different food substances (A, B and C) and records her results in the table shown.

Food substance	Original colour	End colour
A	blue	blue
B	blue	yellow-orange
C	blue	brick red

a State which food substance does not contain a reducing sugar? [1]

....

b State which food substance contained the highest concentration of a reducing sugar. [1]

....

c Explain your reasoning for your answer to part b. [2]

....

d State the name of the solution that Moira used to test for the reducing sugars. [1]

....

e After adding the solution from part d, state what Moira needed to do next. [1]

....

f State one safety precaution that Moira should have taken when testing for reducing sugars. [1]

....

g Suggest the name of a food substance that could have been food substance C in the investigation. [1]

....

Total [8]

2   Describe how you would test whether a sample of food contains protein. [6]

....

....

....

....

....

....

Total [6]

5 Enzymes

Overview

In this chapter, you will investigate factors that affect enzyme activity. You will use your knowledge of enzymes to plan and carry out investigations into how enzymes affect rate of reactions. The results will enhance your knowledge and understanding of how enzyme structure is linked to function.

Practical investigation 5.1 Effect of amylase on starch

Objective

In this investigation, you will observe the effect of the enzyme amylase on starch and test the product of the reaction. This will require you to combine your knowledge of food tests with the structure of carbohydrates.

Equipment

- Test-tubes × 4
- 2% starch solution
- Benedict's solution
- 5% amylase solution
- Test-tube rack
- Bunsen burner
- Marker pen
- Pipettes × 3
- Iodine solution
- Glass beaker (250 ml)
- Safety spectacles
- Tripod
- Gauze mat
- Heat mat
- Disposable gloves

Method

1   Prepare a water bath in the glass beaker using a Bunsen burner, tripod, gauze mat and heat mat.
2   Heat the water to boiling point, then reduce the heat so that the water temperature is just around boiling point.
3   Label the four test-tubes with the marker pen (A, B, C and D) and place them in the test-tube rack.
4   Add 5 ml of the 2% starch solution to each test-tube.
5   Use a different pipette to add 2 ml of the 5% amylase solution to tubes B and D. Gently shake the tubes to mix the contents together and leave for 5 minutes.
6   Add 2–3 drops of iodine solution to test-tubes A and B.
7   Use the third pipette to add 3 ml of Benedict's solution to test-tubes C and D and place both of these test-tubes into the water bath for 5 minutes.

Safety considerations

- Wear safety spectacles at all times.
- Wear gloves or wash hands immediately after handling iodine solution.
- Take care when using the Bunsen burner and water bath. Leave the equipment and water bath to cool for several minutes at the end of the investigation.

Recording data

1 Record your results in the table.

Test-tube	Solutions added	Testing agent used	Colour change
A			
B			
C			
D			

Analysis

2 Suggest a reason for the colour change in test-tube B.

....

3 Describe the colour change in test-tube D.

....

4 Name the nutrient that is present in test-tube D.

....

5 Explain your reason for your answer to Question 3.

....

....

6 Outline the role that amylase played in producing the results in test-tube D.

....

....

....

Evaluation

7 Suggest why it was important to allow the water bath to cool at the end of the investigation?

....

....

8 Korey repeats the experiment with boiled amylase. What effect, if any, do you predict this will have on the results produced for test-tube D? Explain your answer.

....

....

....

....

Practical investigation 5.2 Effect of temperature on enzyme activity

Objective

You will carry out an investigation to observe the effect of temperature on the rate of enzyme activity, and link this to your knowledge of enzyme structure.

Equipment

- 1% starch solution
- Iodine solution
- 5% amylase solution
- Marker pen
- Pipette × 2
- Test-tube rack
- Stopwatch
- Kettle
- 250 ml glass beaker × 3
- Thermometer
- Safety spectacles
- Ice cubes
- Test-tubes × 6

Method

1 Label test-tubes 1–6 and place in the test-tube rack.
2 Place 5 ml of the 1% starch solution into test-tubes 1, 3 and 5.
3 Add three drops of iodine solution to test-tubes 1, 3 and 5.
4 Use a second pipette to add 1 ml of the 5% amylase solution to test-tubes 2, 4 and 6.
5 Prepare a water bath in each of the 250 ml glass beakers as follows:
    - Ice and water at approximately 10 °C
    - Room temperature water at approximately 20–25 °C
    - Water from hot tap (or combined with part-boiled water) at approximately 35–40 °C
6 Place test-tubes 1 and 2 into the cold-water bath, test-tubes 3 and 4 into the room temperature water bath, and test-tubes 5 and 6 into the warm water bath.
7 Leave for 5–10 minutes for the solutions inside the test-tube to match the temperature of the water bath.
8 Pour the amylase solution from test-tube 1 into test-tube 2, gently shake to mix the contents, return to the water bath, and start the stopwatch.
9 Observe and record the time taken for the blue/black colour to disappear and for the solution to become colourless.
10 Repeat steps 8–9 for each of the water baths.

Safety considerations

- Wear safety spectacles at all times.
- Wear gloves or wash hands thorough after using iodine solution.

Recording data

1 Record your results in the table below. You must add the appropriate units to the headings.

Test-tube	Temperature /	Time for the solution to become colourless / ....
1		
3		
5		

Handling data

2 Produce a line graph to show how the time taken for the solution to become colourless was affected by the temperature of the solution. You should use the following as a guide for producing a suitable graph:
   - Axes drawn using a pencil and ruler
   - Axes suitably labelled with appropriate units
   - Independent variable is on the x-axis
   - Dependent variable is on the y-axis
   - Points plotted accurately using a sharp pencil
   - Points joined together by a straight line but not extended

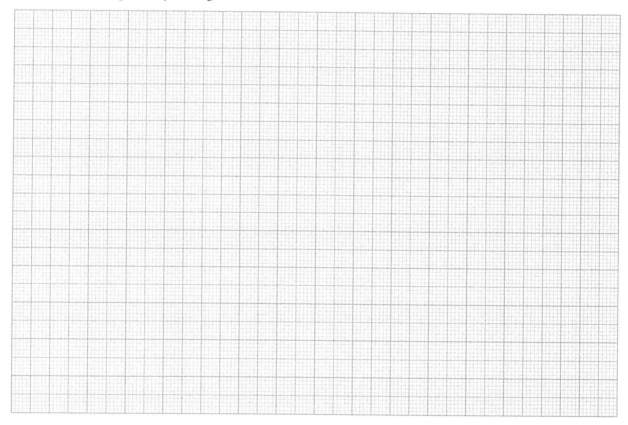

Analysis

3 State the temperature at which the rate of reaction was fastest. ....

4 Explain why the blue colour disappears from the solution.

   ....

   ....

5 Describe how temperature affects the rate of the reaction catalysed by amylase in this investigation.

   ....

   ....

6 Using your line graph, state the time it would take for the blue colour to disappear when the reaction takes place at 70 °C.

....

Evaluation

7 Outline how the validity of this investigation could be improved.

....

....

Practical investigation 5.3 Effect of pH on enzyme activity

Objective

You will plan an investigation into the effect of pH on enzyme activity. You will analyse the data collected and produce a suitable graph to support your findings of how pH affects the rate of reaction of the enzyme.

Equipment

- Spotting tile
- Iodine solution
- Safety spectacles
- Test-tubes ×3, labelled A, B and C
- 1% amylase solution
- 1% starch solution
- Range of buffer solutions
- Pipettes
- Test-tube rack
- Stopwatch

Method

1   Place a drop of iodine solution in each of the dimples of the spotting tile.
2   Add 1 ml of buffer solution to test-tube A.
3   Add 2 ml of the starch solution to test-tube A.
4   Add 2 ml of the amylase solution to test-tube A, mix together and start the clock immediately.
5   Every 10 seconds, remove a drop of the mixture in test-tube A and place this onto one of the iodine drops on the spotting tile. The iodine solution should turn blue/black.
6   Repeat this until the iodine solution no longer turns blue/black.
7   Count the number of iodine drops used and record in the table below.
8   Repeat steps 1–7 using the different buffer solutions available to you.

Safety considerations

- Wear safety spectacles at all times.
- Wear gloves or wash hands after contact with iodine solution.

Recording data

1   Draw and complete your own table to show the number of iodine drops taken until there is no longer a colour change. You should ensure that you include all relevant information and units in the headings. Include one extra column for calculating the time taken for the reaction to take place.

Handling data

2   Each drop of iodine equals 10 seconds for the enzyme to break down the starch. Calculate the time taken for each of the buffer solutions in the end column of your table.

3 Plot a graph (in the space provided) for the time taken for the starch to break down against the different pH used in the buffer solutions.

Analysis

4 Describe the effect that the different pH solutions had on the time taken for starch to be broken down by the amylase solution.

....

....

5 Explain why the pH had an effect on the time taken for the reaction to take place.

....

....

....

Evaluation

6 State why the buffer solution was added before the starch solution.

....

....

7 Suggest one way in which the reliability of the investigation could be improved.

....

....

8 It is possible for different students to count a varied number of drops when observing the colour change of the iodine. How could this potential human source of error be removed from the investigation?

....

....

Exam-style question

1 Figure 5.1 shows the effect of pH on two different enzymes, A and B.

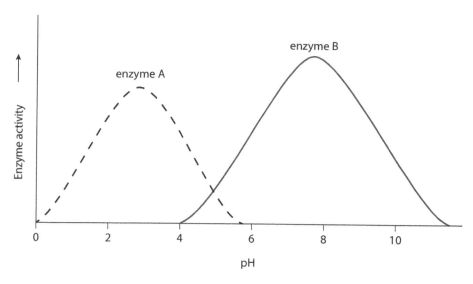

Figure 5.1

a State the optimum pH of enzyme A. [1]

....

b State the optimum pH of enzyme B. [1]

....

c Suggest a part of the body where enzyme A might be found. [1]

....

d Suggest a part of the body where enzyme B might be found. [1]

....

e Suggest and explain what would happen if enzyme A was placed in a solution of pH 8. [3]

....

....

....

....

Total [7]

6 Plant nutrition

Overview

In this chapter, you will investigate factors that affect photosynthesis which will help you better understand the process of photosynthesis. You will calculate the rate of photosynthesis in plants under different conditions and use this data to produce a suitable graph.

Practical investigation 6.1 Testing leaves for the presence of starch

Objective

In this investigation, you will carry out the basic test for starch on leaves. This will provide you with the skills necessary for the investigations later in the chapter where you will plan your own investigations into the rate of photosynthesis.

Equipment

- 250 ml glass beaker
- Bunsen burner
- Tripod
- Gauze mat
- Heat mat
- Test-tube tongs
- Iodine solution
- White tile (or Petri dish)
- Safety spectacles
- Forceps
- Boiling tube
- Alcohol solution
- Leaf

Method

1 Heat at least 100 ml of water in the boiling tube, using the Bunsen burner. Reduce the heat and keep the water at boiling point.
2 Use the forceps to dip the leaf into the water for 10 seconds and turn off the Bunsen burner.
3 Place the leaf in the bottom of the boiling tube and submerge it in alcohol solution.
4 Place the boiling tube into the water bath (this is the glass beaker of boiled water) for at least 5–7 minutes, until the leaf is white or very pale green.
5 Use the test-tube tongs to remove the boiling tube from the water bath.
6 Carefully dispose of the alcohol solution and remove the leaf.
7 Wash the leaf under water for a few seconds before placing it flat on a white tile or surface.
8 Add 2–3 drops of iodine solution to cover the leaf and leave for 2 minutes.
9 Remove any excess iodine with a paper towel or by holding it under a slow-running tap.

Safety considerations

- Wear safety spectacles at all times.

1 Suggest two safety precautions for the use of alcohol, iodine solution and a Bunsen burner.

....

....

....

Recording data

2 Sketch and label a diagram to show what happened to your leaf.

Analysis

3 Why was alcohol used in step 3 of the method?

....

4 Suggest why it was necessary to remove the green colour from the leaf.

....

5 Describe the colour change of the leaf after iodine solution was added.

....

Evaluation

6 Suggest how the amount of starch present in the leaf might be observed in this investigation.

....

....

Practical investigation 6.2 Light as a limiting factor for photosynthesis

Objective

In this investigation, you will use your knowledge of the starch test to plan and carry out an investigation to observe how light is a limiting factor for photosynthesis. You will link the results of the investigation to your knowledge of photosynthesis.

Equipment

1   There are three pieces of equipment in the list below that are not required for this investigation. Use a pencil and ruler to cross them out before you begin.

- One plant per class with foil on parts of the leaves
- Benedict's solution
- Paper clip
- 250 ml glass beaker
- Conical flask
- Bunsen burner
- Tripod
- Gauze mat
- Heat mat

- Test-tube tongs
- Iodine solution
- White tile (or Petri dish)
- Thermometer
- Safety spectacles
- Forceps
- Boiling tube
- Alcohol solution

Method

You have been provided with a plant that has initially been kept in the dark for 48 hours, then had parts of its leaves covered in foil before being left in direct sunlight for at least 6 hours.

2   Plan a method to investigate how the presence and absence of light affects the rate of photosynthesis in the different parts of the leaves.

1   ....

2   ....

3   ....

4   ....

5   ....

6   ....

7   ....

8   ....

9   ....

10 ....

Safety considerations

3 Outline your safety precautions here for your investigation.

....

....

....

....

....

Recording data

4 Sketch and label your leaf at the end of the investigation. Label areas of the leaf that contain starch and areas that do not contain starch.

Analysis

5 What colour did the iodine turn on the part of the leaf that was covered by the aluminium foil?

....

6 Suggest why this colour change occurred.

....

....

Evaluation

7 Why was the plant kept in the dark for 48 hours before placing the aluminium foil on the leaf?

....

....

Practical investigation 6.3 Effect of light intensity on oxygen production in Canadian pondweed

Objective

In this investigation, you will investigate the effect of light intensity on the rate of photosynthesis and generate data to analyse. You will use your knowledge of the factors which affect the rate of photosynthesis to explain the results of the investigation.

Equipment

- Water plant
- Light source
- Stopwatch
- Boiling tube
- Boss clamp and stand
- Metre ruler
- Paper clip

Method

1 Attach the paper clip to the water plant to help anchor the plant when placed into the water.
2 Set up the boiling tube and fill it almost to the top with water. Fix it upright by using the boss clamp and stand.
3 Set the lamp up so that the bulb is 0.6 m away from the boiling tube.
4 Add the water plant to the boiling tube and start the stopwatch.
5 Count the number of bubbles produced by the plant in 1 minute and record in the table.
6 Repeat step 5 two more times.
7 Repeat steps 3–6 at the following distances from the boiling tube: 0.4 m, 0.2 m and 0.0 m.

Safety considerations

Take care when handling the lamp as this will become very hot.

Recording data

1 Record your results in the table.

Distance between plant and light source / m	Number of bubbles in 1 minute			
	Record 1	Record 2	Record 3	Average per minute
0.6				
0.4				
0.2				
0.0				

Handling data

2 Describe how the mean number of bubbles per minute can be calculated.

....

....

3 Draw a line graph to show how the distance between the plant and the light source affected the mean number of bubbles produced.

Analysis

4 Describe the shape of the curve shown in your graph.

....

....

5 Explain why the curve 'straightened' after a certain point.

....

....

Evaluation

6 Suggest why the mean number of bubbles was calculated.

....

....

....

Exam-style question

1   Figure 6.1 shows a variegated leaf.

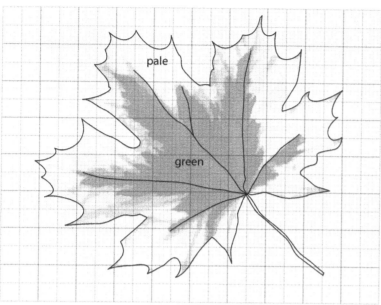

Figure 6.1

a Estimate the size of the leaf in Figure 6.1. Show your working below. [2]

Answer: .... cm²

b Draw a large labelled diagram of the leaf in Figure 6.1. [5]

c Calculate the magnification of the leaf drawn in your diagram. [2]

....

....

....

d The leaf was tested for the presence of starch. Label the part of the leaf that you would predict will turn blue/black in the presence of iodine solution. [1]

e Explain why this area would turn blue/black in the presence of iodine solution. [3]

....

....

Total [13]

7 Animal nutrition

Overview

In this chapter, you will investigate the energy contained in different types of food and how physical and chemical digestion take place in the human body.

Practical investigation 7.1 Measuring the energy content of foodstuffs, part I

Objective

In this investigation, you will investigate the different energy contents of a range of foods from everyday life. You will evaluate the quality of your method and plan a follow-up investigation.

Equipment

- Bunsen burner
- Boss clamp and stand
- Boiling tubes × 4
- Thermometer
- Heat mat
- Water
- Safety spectacles
- Mounted needle
- Samples of food × 4

Method

1   Set up the Bunsen burner and clamp stand as shown in Figure 7.1.

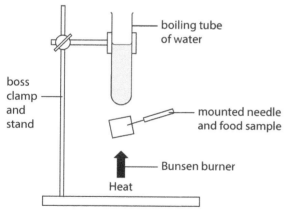

Figure 7.1

2   Fill a boiling tube to approximately halfway up with water.
3   Turn on the Bunsen burner and heat the end of the mounted needle for a few seconds until it glows red.
4   Mount your food sample onto the mounted needle, taking extra care not to burn yourself with the red-hot needle.
5   Record the starting temperature of the water in the boiling tube.

6 Heat the food under the boiling tube until the food stops burning.

7 Record the final temperature of the water.

8 Repeat steps 2–7 with three other food samples.

Safety considerations

- Wear safety spectacles.
- Tie hair back and secure loose items of clothing.
- Do not touch the end of the hot needle, or the boiling tube immediately after burning. Leave the boiling tube to cool or remove using test-tube tongs.

Recording data

1 Record your data in the following table. Complete the table by adding the units to the temperature column heading.

Food sample	Temperature of the water /................................		
	Initial temperature	Final temperature	Change

Analysis

2 State which food had the highest energy content in your investigation.

....

3 Explain how you know that this food had the highest energy content in your investigation.

....

....

Evaluation

Your answers in this section will form the basis of Practical investigation 7.2. Use the information in the question to guide your response to the question.

4 You tested each food sample only once. Describe how you could improve the reliability of your investigation and the data gained from it.

....

....

5 The boiling tube was filled to approximately halfway with water. Describe how the validity of the investigation could be improved.

....

....

6 You may have used different sizes and shapes for your food samples. Describe how you could improve the validity of your investigation.

....

....

7 Step 7 of the method required you to take the temperature of the water at the end of the investigation. Describe two steps that you should take at this stage to ensure that you take a reliable temperature reading of the water.

....

....

Practical investigation 7.2 Measuring the energy content of foodstuffs, part II

Objective

In this investigation, you are expected to repeat Practical investigation 7.1 but with improvements to the method as suggested in the 'Evaluation' section. You will use your data to plot a graph comparing the energy content of the foods tested.

Equipment

1 Using Practical investigation 7.1 as a guide, list the equipment that you require to carry out a reliable method.

- ....
- ....
- ....
- ....

- ....
- ....
- ....
- ....

- ....
- ....
- ....
- ....

Method

2 Using your suggestions from the evaluation of Practical investigation 7.1, plan a suitable method that will allow you to gather valid and reliable data for the energy content of at least four different foods.

....

....

....

....

....

....

....

....

....

....

Safety considerations

3 State three safety precautions that you will take in order to carry out this investigation.

1 ....

....

2 ....

....

3 ....

....

Recording data

4 Plan and prepare a table suitable for collecting the data from your investigation. You will need suitable headings and allow for the number of repeats that you do for each food sample.

Handling data

5 It is possible to calculate the heat energy transferred in each of the foods using the equation $Q = mc\Delta T$.
Q is the heat energy transferred.
m is the mass of the water.
c is the specific heat capacity of water (4.2 J/Kg°C).
ΔT is the temperature change of the water in degrees Celsius.
Use this information to calculate the heat energy transferred from the food to the water for each of your food samples.

Food A: ....

Food B: ....

Food C: ....

Food D: ....

Analysis

6 Which food released the most heat energy when burnt in your investigation?

....

7 Use the data from your investigation to support your answer to Question 6.

....

....

Evaluation

8 You took a reading from the thermometer at eye level at either zero or one decimal place. Suggest how you could improve the accuracy of your temperature reading.

....

....

Practical investigation 7.3 Mouthwash versus acids

Objective

In this investigation, you will observe and compare the differences in an egg placed in two different solutions. You will then relate the results to how a fluoride mouthwash protects the enamel on your teeth from being eroded by the acids in your mouth every day.

Equipment

- Hard-boiled eggs × 2
- Jars with screw-on lids × 2
- Vinegar
- Fluoride mouthwash
- Marker pen
- Disposable gloves
- Safety spectacles

Method

1   Label your jars with your initials.
2   Place one egg in each of the jars.
3   Cover one of the eggs with vinegar and screw the lid on top of the jar.
4   Cover the other egg with fluoride mouthwash and screw the lid on top of the jar.
5   Leave the eggs for at least 24 hours, or until your next lesson.
6   Remove the eggs from the jars and dispose of the solutions left inside.
7   Observe the eggs and sketch a diagram to show the difference in the eggs in the 'Recording data' section.
8   Squeeze the eggs and note the difference in how they feel.

Safety considerations

- Safely dispose of the solution once the egg is removed.
- Wear gloves when removing the egg from the solution.
- Wear safety spectacles.

Recording data

1   Sketch a diagram of each of the eggs in the space below. Label your eggs and the differences between them.

Analysis

2 Describe the differences between the eggs that were placed in the different solutions.

   ....

   ....

3 Discuss what the results of this experiment tell you about how your teeth are affected by acids.

   ....

   ....

4 Discuss how fluoride mouthwash can protect your teeth from decay by acids.

   ....

   ....

Evaluation

5 Suggest why the amount of acid and mouthwash used in this experiment should have been the same for this investigation.

   ....

   ....

Exam-style questions

1 Mansoor measures the energy content of three different foods. He burns a sample of each food in a Bunsen flame and measures the change in temperature of a volume of water above the burning food. He records his results in the table shown.

Food	Starting temperature /			End temperature /			Change in mean temperature / ....
	Attempt 1	Attempt 2	Mean	Attempt 1	Attempt 2	Mean	
X	24	25	24.5	30	35		
Y	24	24	24	73	71		
Z	24	25	24.5	39	48		

a Enter the missing units in the headings of the table. [1]
b Calculate the mean end temperature of each food. [1]
c Calculate the change in mean temperature of each food. [3]
d Suggest one safety precaution that Mansoor might have taken during his investigation. [1]

   ....

e Mansoor tests food Y with Benedict's solution. The result is positive for reducing sugar. Describe the colour change that took place when Mansoor tested the food with the Benedict's solution. [2]

....

f Suggest to which nutrient group food Y belongs. [1]

....

Total [9]

2 Figure 7.2 shows a cross-section of a typical human tooth.

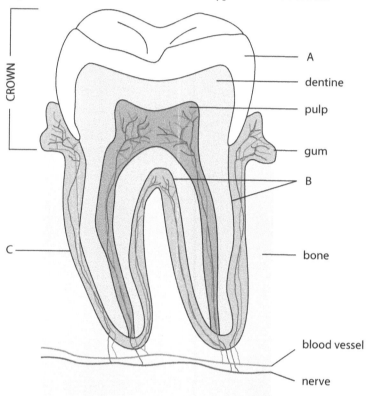

CROWN

A

dentine

pulp

gum

B

bone

blood vessel

nerve

C

Figure 7.2

a Label the missing parts of the tooth.

 i A .... [1]

 ii B .... [1]

 iii C .... [1]

b Describe and explain the effect that sugary drinks will have on the part labelled A. [4]

....

....

....

....

c Outline how teeth can be protected from decay and disease. [4]

....

....

....

....

Total [11]

8 Transport in plants

Overview

In this chapter, you will investigate how water moves in, out and through a plant. You will use your results to calculate the rate at which water enters and exits a plant.

Practical investigation 8.1 Transport of water through plants via xylem

Objective

In this investigation, you will carry out a simple procedure to observe how water moves through a plant and use this to practise your drawing and magnification skills.

Equipment

- Celery stem with leaves attached
- Safety spectacles
- 250 ml glass beaker
- Pipette
- Food colouring/dye
- Scalpel/knife
- Stopwatch/clock

Method

1 Mix a few drops of food colouring with 200 ml of water in the glass beaker.
2 Place the celery stem into the solution and leave for 20 minutes.
3 Remove the celery and cut the stalk in half (or slice a 1 cm piece if sharing with other classmates or groups).
4 Observe and record what you see in the 'Recording data' section.
5 Do not discard your celery stalk – you will need this.

Safety considerations

- Wear safety spectacles.
- Handle the scalpel/knife with care.

Recording data

1 Sketch a large diagram of a cross-section of your celery stem. You may use colour in this diagram to represent any changes in colour that you observe. Label your diagram.

Handling data

2 Calculate the magnification of your drawing compared to your original piece of celery. Show your working in the space below.

Magnification: ....

Analysis

3 State the name of the structure that your water dye has travelled through.

....

4 Outline how this structure provides strength to the plant.

....

....

5 What useful molecules are dissolved in the water that travels up through this structure?

....

Evaluation

6 Joelle decides to repeat your investigation using three different types of plant. Outline why Joelle's investigation is more reliable than yours.

....

....

7 Suggest why food colouring or dye was used in the water.

....

....

Practical investigation 8.2 Testing the product of transpiration

Objective

In this investigation, you will observe that the process of transpiration results in water evaporating from the surface of plant leaves.

Equipment

- Potted plant
- Clear polythene bag
- String or cable tie
- Anhydrous copper sulfate
- Spatula
- Pipette
- Safety spectacles

Method

Steps 1 and 2 have been done in advance for you by the teacher.

1   Place the transparent bag over the plant and tie the bottom of the bag close to the bottom of the plant with the cable tie or string. Tie it firmly.
2   Water the soil and place the plant in direct sunlight for at least 12 hours (this may be overnight).
3   Describe what you can see inside the bag after this time.
4   Remove the bag without spilling the contents – do this by holding the bag with the open end facing upwards.
5   The solution inside the bag should collect in the corner of the bag. Remove some of the solution with the pipette.
6   Add the solution to the anhydrous copper sulfate and record your results.

Safety considerations

Wear safety spectacles and wash hands after contact with anhydrous copper sulfate.

Recording data

1   Describe the changes seen inside the bag.

   ....

   ....

2   Describe what happened to the anhydrous copper sulfate when the solution was placed on it.

   ....

   ....

Analysis

3   What does the change to the anhydrous copper sulfate tell you about the identity of the solution?

   ....

   ....

4 Define transpiration.

....

....

Evaluation

5 Outline the design of an investigation to compare the different rates of transpiration of two different plant types.

....

....

....

....

....

....

Practical investigation 8.3 How environmental factors affect the rate of transpiration

Objective

In this investigation, you will set up a potometer to investigate the rate of water uptake by plants placed under different environmental conditions. This provides an indication of the rate of transpiration and you will record your results on a graph.

Equipment

- Potometer
- Leafy plant
- Electric fan
- Ruler
- Petroleum jelly (or similar)

Method

1   Set up the potometer and plant as shown in Figure 8.1.

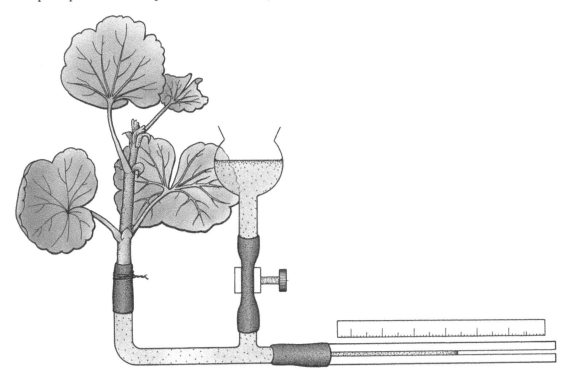

Figure 8.1

2   Ensure that there are no air gaps between the plant and the potometer tubing. Your teacher will provide you with a substance such as petroleum jelly to seal any gaps.
3   Open the clip and fill the tubing with the water. Close the clip immediately.
4   Place the plants in different conditions – one with an electric fan blowing onto the plant, one on the shelf or by the window, and one in a dark corner of the room – for 15 minutes at a time.
5   Record the position of the water meniscus every minute for 15 minutes in the table in the 'Recording data' section.

Safety considerations

Take care when handling glass and fixing the tubing to the end of the plant.

Recording data

1 Draw a table that records the amount of water drawn into the plant (ml) every minute for 15 minutes under the three different sets of conditions. Your table must include relevant headings and units.

Handling data

2 Produce a graph to show the amount of water taken in by the plant per minute under each of the three conditions.

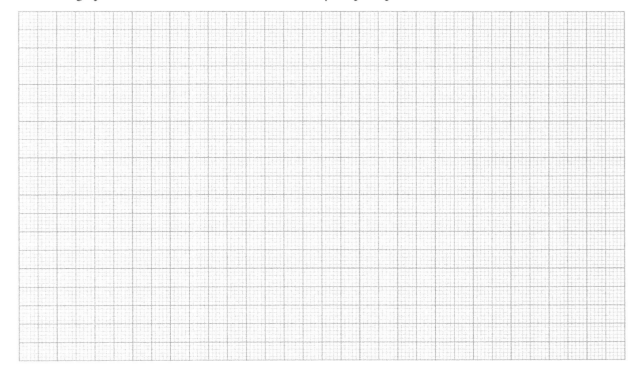

Analysis

3 Under which condition did the plant take up the most water?

....

4 Suggest a reason for the increase in water uptake under these conditions.

....

....

5 Outline why the rate of water uptake is an indicator of the rate of transpiration in a plant.

....

....

Evaluation

6 State the independent variable in this investigation.

....

7 State the dependent variable in this investigation.

....

8 Outline the control variables for this investigation.

....

....

Exam-style questions

1 Describe the pathway that a molecule of water might take from the soil to when it leaves the plant because of transpiration. [5]

....

....

....

....

....

Total [5]

2 Look at Figure 8.2 below and answer the questions that follow.

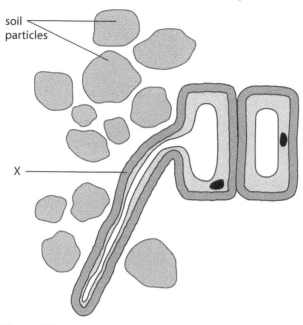

soil particles

X

Figure 8.2

a Describe and explain how the structure labelled X allows a plant root to absorb as much water as the plant requires. [3]

....

....

....

....

b The structure labelled X absorbs water from the soil by osmosis. Describe and explain how osmosis enables the plant to take in water from the soil. [3]

....

....

....

c Sucrose is transported from its source to other parts of the plant. State the name of one place where this sucrose may be translocated to. [1]

....

Total [7]

9 Transport in animals

Overview

In this chapter, you will observe how the heart and lungs are structured, and how they contribute to the well-being of the body by supplying organs with the substances that they require. You will link your knowledge of these organs to how they respond under different conditions.

Practical investigation 9.1 Dissecting a heart

Objective

In this investigation, you will dissect and draw the heart of a mammal to identify the different parts. You will evaluate the safety precautions taken during this investigation.

Equipment

- Heart of a mammal
- Scalpel
- Latex gloves
- White tile or dissection tray
- Paper towels
- Water
- Pipette or syringe
- Forceps
- Safety spectacles
- Mounted needle
- Surgical scissors
- Aprons

Method

1   Prepare your working area as directed by your teacher. You should have paper towels under and around your white tile for cutting (if you are not using a dissection tray or similar container).
2   Wear the gloves, apron and safety spectacles.
3   Examine the heart to identify the major parts such as the major blood vessels and the ventricles. The left-hand side of the heart will feel firmer than the right-hand side as it is more muscular.
4   There are two different methods to dissect the heart. You can try either one of the methods listed below.
5   You will need to sketch at least one drawing of the inside of the heart and record it in the 'Recording data' section.

Method A

1 Use a pair of surgical scissors to cut a horizontal slice at the top of the heart. See 'cut 1' in Figure 9.1 for guidance.

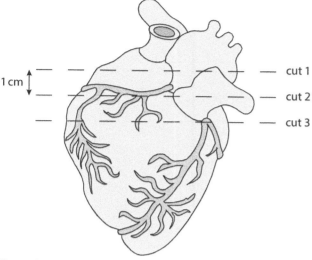

Figure 9.1

2 Examine the internal structure of the heart and take a photograph if you have a suitable device to do so. You can label the photograph at a later stage.

3 Repeat the cut a further 1 cm down (see 'cut 2' in Figure 9.1) the heart and examine again, taking a photograph if you have a suitable device to do so.

4 Use the water and pipette/syringe to send water through the blood vessels and observe the route that the water takes.

5 Repeat the 1 cm slices until you have viewed most of the internal structures of the heart.

6 Clear away your equipment and heart as directed by your teacher, following the safety and disposal guidelines.

Method B

1 Place the heart on the table/tile/dissection tray so that it is lying flat.

2 Make a longitudinal cut (with the scalpel or scissors) along the side of the heart, slicing carefully through to the opposite side – but do NOT cut all the way through. Your hand should remain pressed on the top of the heart to keep it in place.

3 The heart should now open up like a book for you to view the inside. Inspect the walls of the left and right ventricles and annotate your diagram with any differences in thickness of the walls that you can see. Depending on where the heart was sourced from, you may be able to observe blood vessels that are intact.

4 Examine the heart for other structures and features, such as coronary blood vessels, cardiac muscle and fatty deposits.

Safety considerations

- Wear safety spectacles, gloves and an apron at all times.
- Wash hands and surfaces after completion of the investigation. Your teacher will instruct the laboratory technician to clean the surfaces with disinfectant.
- Do not eat or drink in the laboratory.
- Take care when handling and using the scalpel and scissors.

Recording data

1   Make a large drawing of your cross-section of the heart. Label as many different parts of the heart that you can observe. You may be able to see some, or all, of the following parts: aorta, pulmonary vein, atrial wall, valve tendons, valve flaps, left ventricle wall, right ventricle wall, septum.

Evaluation

2   For each of the following safety precautions, outline why they were taken for this investigation.

   a Wearing gloves and an apron

   ....
   ....

   b Washing hands

   ....
   ....

   c Cleaning the surface with disinfectant

   ....
   ....

   d Not eating or drinking in the laboratory

   ....
   ....

Practical investigation 9.2 Effect of exercise on heart rate, part I

Objective

In this investigation, you will plan and investigate how different levels of exercise affect your heart rate.

Equipment

- Stopwatch
- Area to exercise

Method

1 Read the method with your group and plan a suitable table in the 'Recording data' section.
2 Remain at rest for at least 1 minute.
3 Measure your pulse on your wrist or your neck for 30 seconds. Your teacher will demonstrate how to do this. Count the number of beats in 30 seconds then multiply by two to get your heart rate per minute. This provides you with the unit for this measurement; your 'beats per minute' of the heart.
4 Exercise lightly for 1 minute and record your pulse afterwards.
5 Sit down until your pulse returns to its original resting rate as recorded in step 3.
6 Exercise vigorously for 1 minute and record your pulse.
7 Repeat steps 2–6 with the different members of your group.

Safety considerations

- Clear a suitable space for your chosen exercise or activity and be aware of any potential trip hazards.
- Drink water and rest if you feel unwell at any point.

Recording data

1 Draw a table to record the following for each member of your group:
   - Resting heart rate
   - Heart rate after light exercise
   - Heart rate after heavy exercise

Handling data

2 Calculate your change in heart rate from resting after each type of exercise.
After light exercise:

....

....

After heavy exercise:

....

....

Analysis

3 Describe the effect that exercise has had on your heart rate.

....

....

4 Explain why your heart rate increased during exercise.

....

....

Evaluation

5 Suggest a more accurate method for measuring your pulse or heart rate.

....

Practical investigation 9.3 Effect of exercise on heart rate, part II

Objective

In this investigation, you will plan an investigation on how your heart rate is affected by exercise over longer periods of time. You will use the data gathered in the investigation to plot a graph of your results.

Equipment

- Stopwatch
- Area to exercise

Method

1 Plan a method to measure your heart rate:
   - before exercise
   - after 1 minute of exercise
   - after 3 minutes of exercise
   - after 5 minutes of exercise

....

....

....

....

....

....

....

....

Safety considerations

2 Outline two safety precautions that you should take for your investigation.

....

....

Recording data

3 Draw a table below to record your investigation results, including all headings and units.

Handling data

4 Plot a graph to show the change in heart rate in your investigation.

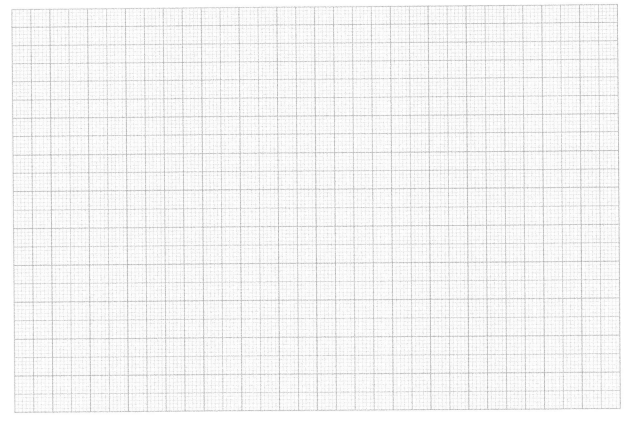

Analysis

5 Describe the effect that exercise has had on your heart rate.

....

....

6 Explain why your heart rate increased during exercise.

....

....

Exam-style question

1 Kelse is carrying out a heart dissection for his biology class and accidentally cuts his finger while using the scalpel. He washes his finger under cold water, allowing the wound to bleed out, before applying a plaster to the cut.

a Suggest why Kelse ran water over the cut for a few minutes. [2]

....

....

b The blood begins to clot after several minutes. Outline why blood clotting is useful to Kelse in this situation. [2]

....

....

c State the name of the insoluble protein that forms fibres, creating a mesh over Kelse's cut. [1]

....

d A blood clot is made up of trapped red blood cells under a mesh of fibrin. Explain why red blood cells are usually slightly larger in diameter than the capillaries. [3]

....

....

e Blood transports many other useful substances around the body. State the name of three useful substances that are carried around the body in blood. [3]

....

....

....

Total [11]

10 Pathogens and immunity

Overview

In this chapter, you will investigate the bacteria which are present in your surroundings and link this to how the human body protects against pathogenic organisms entering the body. Knowledge of these procedures is important in protecting yourself from pathogenic organisms that are around you.

Practical investigation 10.1 Culturing bacteria

Objective

The aim of this investigation is to become familiar with the safety techniques required and the potential danger that incorrect use in the laboratory poses to all students and teachers.

Equipment

- Disinfectant
- Sterile agar plate (Petri dish)
- Marker pen
- Incubator
- Microbe sample in nutrient broth
- Bunsen burner and heat mat
- Safety spectacles
- Inoculating loop
- Sticky tape

Method

1 Wash your hands with soap and water and ensure your workbench is cleaned with the disinfectant.
2 Label the sterile agar plate with your name.
3 Turn on your Bunsen burner and use the hotter flame for the next steps.
4 Heat the inoculating loop until it is glowing red-hot.
5 Unscrew the bottle of nutrient broth containing the microbe sample and hold the opening of the bottle in the flame for 2–3 seconds.
6 Turn off the Bunsen burner.
7 Place the loop into the microbe sample and replace the lid on the bottle.
8 Lift the lid of the Petri dish so that you can just fit the inoculating loop inside. Gently move the loop over the surface of the agar and replace the lid.

9 Seal the Petri dish with the sticky tape, as shown in Figure 10.1.

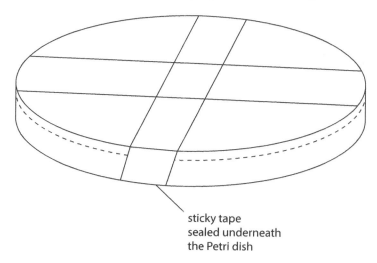

sticky tape
sealed underneath
the Petri dish

Figure 10.1

10 Place the dish upside down in the incubator at 25 °C for 2 days (or your next lesson if this is the next day or after a weekend).

11 Wash your hands with soap and water and clean your workbench with the disinfectant.

12 **DO NOT OPEN THE SEALED PETRI DISH AT ANY POINT.**

13 When you get your Petri dish back, observe what has happened inside. Make a labelled drawing of what you see in the 'Recording data' section.

Safety considerations

- Wear safety spectacles at all times.
- Clean all equipment with disinfectant or similar solution, before and after the investigation.
- Do not open the sealed Petri dish.
- Take care when setting up and using the Bunsen burner.
- Do not eat or drink in the laboratory.
- Do not ingest or inhale the contents of the Petri dish or the bottle of nutrient broth.
- Follow your teacher's safety advice closely during the safety brief and demonstration.
- Cover all open wounds or cuts.

Recording data

1 Make a labelled drawing of what you can see on your Petri dish after 2 days.

Handling data

2 Suggest how you could count the number of different bacterial colonies on your Petri dish.

....

....

3 Estimate the number of bacterial colonies on your Petri dish.

....

Analysis

4 Outline the ideal conditions used in this investigation to cultivate so many bacteria.

....

....

5 Predict what would happen if the Petri dish had been kept at 0°C for 2 days.

....

Evaluation

6 Suggest why the workbench was cleaned with disinfectant and why the inoculating loop was held in the flame of the Bunsen burner at the beginning of the investigation.

....

7 Suggest why it would have been dangerous to incubate the bacteria at 37°C for 2 days.

....

8 Outline why the Petri dish must not be opened once it has been sealed.

....

....

Practical investigation 10.2 Bacteria around you

Objective

In this investigation, you will use the skills learnt in Practical investigation 10.1 to investigate the bacteria of your surroundings. You will ensure that you follow safety precautions to do this as safely as possible.

Equipment

- Safety spectacles
- Disinfectant
- Sterile agar plate (Petri dish)
- Marker pen
- Incubator
- Bunsen burner and heat mat
- Inoculating loop
- Sticky tape

Method

1   Complete the method by entering the correct words in the empty spaces.

    1   Wash your hands with .... and clean your workbench with the ....

    2   Label the sterile agar plate with your ....

    3   Turn on your .... burner and use the hotter flame for the next steps.

    4   Heat the .... until it is glowing red-hot.

    5   Turn off the Bunsen burner.

    6   Collect bacteria from an area of the classroom, such as dirty work surface, door handle or from the top of a cupboard. **Do not collect bacteria from toilets, sinks, spots, noses, mouths or any other source of pathogenic bacteria.**

    7   Lift the lid of the .... dish so that you can just fit the inoculating loop inside. Gently move the loop over the surface of the .... and replace the lid.

    8   Seal the Petri dish with the sticky tape.

    9   Place the dish upside down in the incubator at .... °C for 2 days (or your next lesson if this is the next day or after the weekend).

    10   Wash your hands with soap and water and clean your .... with the disinfectant.

    11   **DO NOT OPEN THE SEALED PETRI DISH AT ANY POINT.**

    12   When you get your Petri dish back, observe what has happened inside. Make a labelled drawing of what you see in the 'Recording data' section.

Safety considerations

- Wear safety spectacles at all times.
- Clean all equipment with disinfectant or similar solution, before and after the investigation.
- **DO NOT OPEN THE SEALED PETRI DISH AT ANY POINT.**
- Take care when setting up and using the Bunsen burner.
- Do not eat or drink in the laboratory.
- Do not ingest or inhale the contents of the Petri dish or the bottle of nutrient broth.
- Cover all open wounds or cuts.

Recording data

2   Make a labelled drawing of what you can observe in your Petri dish after incubation.

Handling data

3   Before you count them, estimate the number of bacterial colonies produced from your chosen area.

    ....

4   Now, count the number of bacterial colonies in your Petri dish.

    ....

Analysis

5   From where in the classroom did you collect your sample with the inoculating loop?

    ....

6   Describe what you observed in your Petri dish.

    ....

Evaluation

7   Describe and explain the safety precautions that you took for this investigation.

    ....
    ....
    ....
    ....
    ....
    ....
    ....

Practical investigation 10.3 Effectiveness of antibacterial mouthwashes on bacteria

Objective

In this investigation, you will observe how three different antibacterial mouthwashes affect a bacterial culture under ideal conditions. You will link this to how the body can be protected from disease and infection.

Equipment

- Disinfectant
- Safety spectacles
- Ruler
- Sterile agar plate (Petri dish)
- Marker pen
- Microbe sample in nutrient broth
- Incubator
- Paper discs
- Antibacterial mouthwash × 3
- Bunsen burner and heat mat
- Inoculating loop
- Sticky tape

Method

1 Wash your hands with soap and water and ensure your workbench is cleaned with the disinfectant.
2 If your teacher has not prepared the paper discs for you in advance, soak them (use the circles from a hole punch) in the three different antibacterial mouthwashes (labelled X Y, and Z). Soak one disc in water as a control.
3 Label the sterile agar plate with your name.
4 Turn on your Bunsen burner and use the hotter, blue flame for the next steps.
5 Heat the inoculating loop until it is glowing red-hot.
6 Unscrew the bottle of nutrient broth containing the microbe sample and hold the opening of the bottle in the flame for 2–3 seconds.
7 Turn off the Bunsen burner.
8 Place the loop into the microbe sample and replace the lid on the bottle.
9 Lift the lid of the Petri dish so that you can just fit the inoculating loop inside. Gently move the loop over the surface of the agar and replace the lid.
10 Place one of each of the discs (X, Y, Z and the control) onto the agar plate. Sketch a diagram to record where each disc is located on the agar.
11 Seal the Petri dish with the sticky tape.
12 Place the dish upside down in the incubator at 25 °C for 2 days (or your next lesson if this is the next day or after the weekend).
13 Wash your hands with soap and water and clean your workbench with the disinfectant.
14 **DO NOT OPEN THE SEALED PETRI DISH AT ANY POINT.**
15 When you get your Petri dish back, observe what has happened inside. Make a labelled drawing of what you see in the 'Recording data' section.

Safety considerations

- Wear safety spectacles at all times.
- Clean all equipment with disinfectant or similar solution, before and after the investigation.
- **DO NOT OPEN THE SEALED PETRI DISH AT ANY POINT.**
- Take care when setting up and using the Bunsen burner.
- Do not eat or drink in the laboratory.
- Do not ingest or inhale the contents of the Petri dish or the bottle of nutrient broth.
- Cover all open wounds or cuts.

Recording data

1   State the name of the solution that each disc was placed in.
    - Disc X

    ....

    - Disc Y

    ....

    - Disc Z

    ....

    - Control disc

    ....

2   Draw and label what happened in your Petri dish after 48 hours in the incubator.

Handling data

3   Without opening the dish, measure the diameter of the clear zone around each disc.
    a Disc X

    ....

    b Disc Y

    ....

    c Disc Z

    ....

    d Control disc

    ....

Analysis

4 State the name of the disc that had the largest diameter clear zone.

....

5 Suggest why this disc had the largest diameter clear zone.

....

....

6 Explain how antibacterial mouthwashes protect the body from disease and infection.

....

....

....

Evaluation

7 What was the purpose of the control disc soaked in water for this investigation?

....

....

Exam-style questions

1 Define the term **pathogen**. [2]

....

....

Total [2]

2 Outline the mechanisms by which our bodies attempt to prevent pathogens from entering. [3]

....

....

....

....

Total [3]

3   Jordan visits the doctor before travelling to another country. The doctor provides Jordan with a vaccination.

a State the purpose of a vaccination. [2]

....

....

b Outline how the vaccination will protect Jordan from disease while he is travelling. [4]

....

....

....

....

Total [6]

11 Respiration and gas exchange

In this chapter, you will investigate the action of respiration under different conditions, as well as how this affects the rate of gaseous exchange. This will provide you with the understanding of how aerobic respiration and anaerobic respiration benefit organisms.

Practical investigation 11.1 Germinating peas

Objective

In this investigation, you will investigate the energy released by germinating peas and compare this to a control sample of peas that are not germinating.

Equipment

- Vacuum flask × 2
- Cotton wool strips
- Thermometer × 2
- Peas, soaked in water for 24 hours
- Peas, boiled
- Dilute disinfectant

Method

1 Wash both sets of peas in the dilute disinfectant.
2 Fill flask A with soaked peas and flask B with boiled peas.
3 Place the thermometer into the middle of the peas and secure this by using the cotton wool to line the inside of the neck of the flask (Figure 11.1).

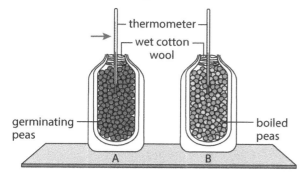

Figure 11.1

4 Record the starting temperature of each flask.
5 Place each flask upside down and record the temperature at the time intervals suggested by your teacher.

Safety considerations

Wash peas in disinfectant to prevent growth of bacteria and fungi.

Recording data

1 Produce a table to record the starting temperature and change in temperature of both sets of peas. Use suitable headings and units in your table.

Handling data

2 Use the following space to calculate the change in temperature for both sets of peas.

    a Boiled peas: ....

    b Germinating peas: ....

Analysis

3 State the difference in temperature change between the boiled peas and the germinating peas.

....

4 Suggest one reason for the increase in temperature.

....

....

Evaluation

5 Explain why the flasks were insulated for the investigation.

....

....

6 Explain the purpose of the boiled peas in this investigation.

....

....

7 Other than safety, suggest why the seeds were disinfected before the start of the investigation.

....

....

8 Outline how you could use the results of your classmates to improve the reliability of your investigation.

....

....

Practical investigation 11.2 Lung dissection

Objective

In this investigation, you will use the dissection skills from Practical investigation 9.1 to dissect and observe the lung of a mammal. You will observe the different parts of the respiratory system and discuss the change in surface area when a lung is inflated.

Equipment

- Lung of a mammal
- Clear plastic tubing
- Dissection tray
- Scalpel
- Dissection scissors
- Disposable gloves
- Safety spectacles

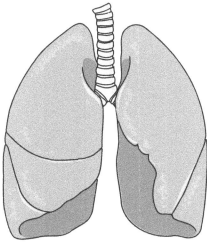

Figure 11.2

Method

1 Prepare your dissection area and the equipment required.
2 Feel the lungs and observe the different features and size.
3 Identify the different areas that you can see with the naked eye. You should be able to see the trachea, the C-shaped tracheal rings, the bronchi, the bronchioles, the pleural membrane, and possibly some of the blood vessels that travel to and from the heart.
4 Your teacher will demonstrate steps 5–6.
5 Insert the plastic tubing down the trachea into one of the lungs.
6 Take a deep breath and blow firmly into the tubing to inflate the lungs. Be careful not to suck, only blow through the tubing.
7 Observe the difference in size of the inflated lung compared to before inflation.
8 Use the dissection tools to remove pieces of lung tissue and examine the structure closely. Make a labelled drawing of your lung specimen in the 'Recording data' section.
9 Place a piece of lung into water and observe what happens.
10 Clear away all equipment and materials as directed by your teacher.

Safety considerations

- Wear safety spectacles and gloves.
- Wash hands after completion of the investigation.
- Take care using the dissection tools.
- Do not eat or drink in the laboratory.

Recording data

1   Make a labelled diagram of the section of lung removed in step 8 of the method.

Analysis

2   **a**   Describe what happened to the piece of lung that you placed into water.

....

....

b   Suggest why this happened to the lung tissue when placed in water.

....

....

Evaluation

3   Suggest and explain what your teacher should do to your work surface to ensure the safety of the next class.

4   Outline how you could compare the difference in size of the inflated lung compared to when it was not inflated.

Practical investigation 11.3 Effect of exercise on breathing rate

Objective

In this investigation, you will plan an investigation on how your breathing rate is affected by exercise over time. You will use the data gathered in the investigation to plot a graph of your results.

Equipment

- Stopwatch
- Area to exercise

Method

1   Plan a method to measure your breathing rate:
    - before exercise
    - after 1 minute of exercise
    - after 3 minutes of exercise
    - after 5 minutes of exercise

    ....

    ....

    ....

    ....

    ....

    ....

    ....

    ....

Safety considerations

2   Outline two safety precautions that you should take for your investigation.

    ....

    ....

Recording data

3   Draw a table below to record your results for the investigation, including all headings and units.

Handling data

4 Plot a graph to show the change in breathing rate in your investigation.

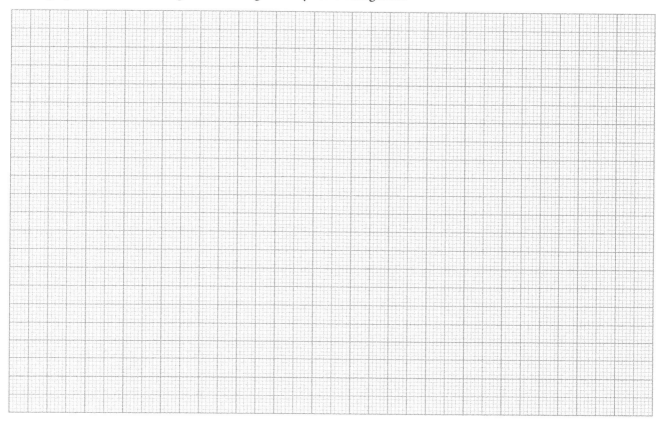

Analysis

5 Describe the effect that the exercise had on your breathing rate.

....

....

6 Explain why your breathing rate increased after exercise.

....

....

Practical investigation 11.4 Repaying the oxygen debt

Objective

In this investigation, you will plan an investigation to observe the time required to repay the oxygen debt after exercise. You will use your results to compare the different recovery periods of different students and explain the purpose of this recovery period.

Equipment

- Stopwatch
- Activity area

Method

1 Plan a method that incorporates the following:
   - measuring breathing rate before exercise
   - vigorous exercise that will cause muscles to begin to ache
   - measuring of breathing rate every minute after exercise until breathing rate returns to the resting rate.

   You may use Practical investigation 11.3 to help guide your plan.

   ....
   ....
   ....
   ....
   ....
   ....
   ....
   ....
   ....
   ....

Safety considerations

- Stop exercise if feeling unwell or dizzy.
- Drink water during and after exercise as required.
- Clear sufficient space for safe exercise with no tripping hazards.

Recording data

2   Produce a table to record your breathing rate at rest, your breathing rate every minute after exercise, and the number of minutes required to return to the resting breathing rate. Use appropriate headings and units for your table.

Handling data

3   Plot a line graph to show the change in breathing rate from the resting period to when the rate returns to the resting rate after exercise.

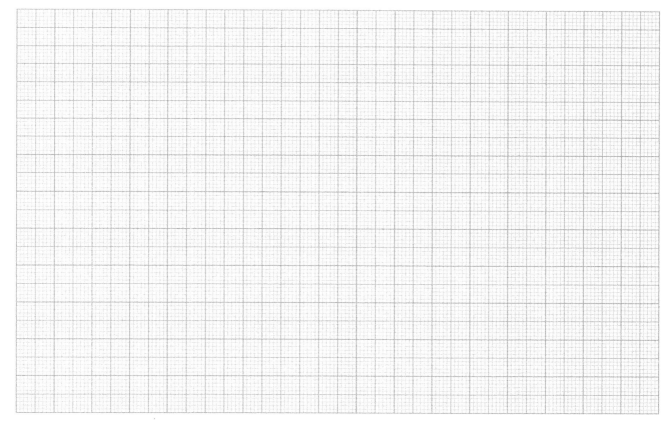

Analysis

4   Describe the changes in breathing rate from the start to finish of this investigation.

....

....

....

5   Explain why the breathing rate remained higher than the resting breathing rate after the exercise had finished.

....

....

....

6   State the name of the substance that caused your muscles to ache during the exercise.

....

7   Define what the **recovery period** is in this investigation.

....

....

Evaluation

8   Suggest why the exercise should stop immediately if the volunteer feels unwell or dizzy.

....

....

Exam-style questions

1 Figure 11.3 shows a recording taken during breathing.

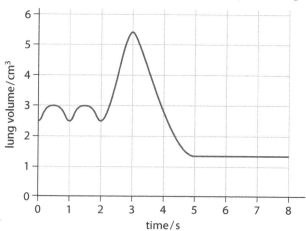

Figure 11.3

a Describe what is happening in the first 2 seconds. [1]

....

....

b State what happens between 2 seconds and 3 seconds. [1]

....

c State the name of the volume at 6 seconds. [1]

....

d Calculate the tidal volume of the normal breaths. Show your working. [3]

....

....

e Calculate the volume of the air taken during the deep breath. [3]

....

....

Total [9]

2 Melissa runs 5 km every morning. Describe and explain how her breathing rate would change during the course of her run. [4]

....

....

....

....

Total [4]

3 a Define **aerobic respiration**. [4]

....

....

b State the balanced chemical equation for aerobic respiration. [3]

....

Total [7]

4 a Define **anaerobic respiration**. [4]

....

....

b State the balanced equation for anaerobic respiration in yeast. [3]

....

Total [7]

5 Sam is relaxing at home and decides that he is going to go for a run as part of his attempt to be fit and healthy. Sam has been sitting for 3 minutes but then runs for 7 minutes until the muscles in his legs begin to ache.
He sits down for 4 minutes until his breathing rate returns to normal.

a Sketch a graph to show how Sam's breathing rate might change over time in the paragraph described above. [3]

b Describe the change in breathing rate for Sam. [2]

....

....

c Explain why Sam's breathing rate did not return to normal until 4 minutes after he finished exercising. [4]

....

....

....

Total [9]

12 Excretion

Overview

In this chapter, you will investigate how the body removes some waste products such as carbon dioxide, as well as those excreted in faeces and urine. The removal of carbon dioxide continues on from what you learnt in Chapter 11.

Practical investigation 12.1 Kidney dissection

Objective

In this investigation, you will dissect a mammal kidney, draw and label the kidney, and use this to calculate the magnification of your drawing compared to the actual kidney.

Equipment

- Kidney of a mammal
- Dissection tray
- Dissection scissors
- Scalpel
- Latex gloves
- Ruler
- Safety spectacles
- Weighing balance

Method

1 Prepare your dissection area and collect the equipment that you will need.
2 Examine the external appearance of the kidney. Identify the structures that you can see. These may include the ureter, renal artery and renal vein.
3 Record the mass and the length of the kidney.
4 Place the kidney on its flat side and place your palm on top of the kidney to hold it steady.
5 Use the scalpel to cut through the kidney from the side until you almost reach the opposite side of the kidney.
6 You can now open the kidney like a book to reveal the internal structures of the kidney.
7 Make a large, labelled drawing of your kidney in the 'Recording data' section.

Safety considerations

1 Devise a safety plan for this investigation.

....

....

....

Recording data

2 Record the following information:

   a Mass of kidney: ....

   b Length of kidney: ....

   c Labelled drawing of the internal structures of the kidney.

Handling data

3 Calculate the magnification of your drawing compared to the kidney that you dissected.

   Magnification: ....

Analysis

4 Select one of the internal structures that you can see in your dissected kidney. Describe the function of this structure.

   ....

   ....

   ....

Evaluation

5 Not all of the internal structures of the kidney could be seen with the naked eye. Suggest how structures such as the nephrons could be viewed.

   ....

   ....

   ....

Practical investigation 12.2 Expired and inspired air

Objective

In this investigation, you will investigate the differences in composition between expired and inspired air. This is limited to oxygen, carbon dioxide and water vapour but this investigation will observe temperature. This investigation will remind you of the basic tests for carbon dioxide and oxygen.

Equipment

- Safety spectacles
- Thermometer
- Mirror
- Boiling tube

- Plastic straws
- Paper towel
- Limewater
- Cobalt chloride paper

- Wooden splint
- Matches

Method

For each of the steps below (a–d) you will need to record your observations. Read the method carefully.

a Record the temperature of a thermometer. Blow gently onto the thermometer. Record the temperature again.

b Exhale lightly onto the mirror. Test the vapour with the cobalt chloride paper and record your results.

c Pour limewater into the boiling tube to about a third of the way up. Pierce a paper towel with the straw and use the paper towel as a makeshift lid to the boiling tube. Blow gently through the straw into the limewater for 10–15 seconds and record the change.

d Light a wooden splint and extinguish the flame but allow it to remain glowing. Exhale lightly onto the glowing splint and record your observations.

Safety considerations

- Wear safety spectacles.
- Be careful not to suck up the limewater into your mouth. Wash your mouth immediately and seek medical attention if you ingest the limewater.

Recording data

1 For each of the tests, record your observations in the spaces below.

    a Blow onto thermometer

    ....

    b Exhale onto mirror

    ....

    c Blow into limewater

    ....

    d Exhale on glowing splint

    ....

Analysis

2 Explain the results for each of the tests.

  a Blow onto thermometer

  ....

  b Exhale onto mirror

  ....

  c Blow into limewater

  ....

  d Exhale on glowing splint

  ....

Exam-style questions

1 **a** The liver is responsible for deamination. Define **deamination**. [2]

  ....

  ....

  The table below outlines some of the stages of how the liver makes urea.

Stage	Letter
Useful amino acids released back into the circulation	A
Urea removed from the liver and transported away by the blood	B
Ammonia converted into urea	C
Amino acids taken into the liver by the hepatic portal vein	D
Amino acids deaminated into carbohydrates and ammonia	E

  b Place the letters from the table in the correct order that they occur in the liver as urea is made. [5]

  ....

Total [7]

2 Outline the advantages of a patient receiving a kidney transplant rather than kidney dialysis. [3]

  ....

  ....

  ....

  ....

Total [3]

13 Coordination and response

Overview

In this chapter, you will investigate how the human body reacts to different stimuli and link this to the purpose of voluntary and involuntary reactions.

Practical investigation 13.1 Measuring reaction times

Objective

You will investigate your own reaction time whilst catching a falling object. You will need to make a plan of how you are going to record your results. You will also consider the impact of anticipation on your reaction time.

Equipment

- Half-metre ruler
- Table or bench to rest arm on

Method

1   Work in pairs for this investigation, reversing roles when the method is complete. Discuss your investigation and sketch a table in the 'Recording data' section before you begin.
2   Student A rests their arm on a table or lab bench with their hand hanging free.
3   Student B places the ruler between the forefinger and thumb but not touching the fingers at all with the 0 of the ruler lined up with the forefinger and thumb.
4   When student B lets go of the ruler, student A must catch it between their forefinger and thumb.
5   Record the distance that the ruler was caught by student A.
6   Repeat steps 2–5 three more times.
7   Reverse roles for students A and B and repeat steps 2–6.

Safety considerations

If using a wooden ruler, check that the ruler does not have fragments of wood sticking out that may cause minor cuts or splinters.

Recording data

1 Plan and draw a table to record the results for you and your partner. Include a column to calculate the mean for the distance caught.

Handling data

2 Use the data in this table to calculate the reaction time for you and your partner's mean distance caught.

Distance/mm	Time/s	Distance/mm	Time/s	Distance/mm	Time/s
10	0.045	140	0.169	270	0.235
20	0.064	150	0.175	280	0.239
30	0.078	160	0.181	290	0.243
40	0.09	170	0.186	300	0.247
50	0.102	180	0.192	310	0.252
60	0.111	190	0.197	320	0.256
70	0.12	200	0.202	330	0.26
80	0.128	210	0.207	340	0.263
90	0.136	220	0.212	350	0.267
100	0.143	230	0.217	360	0.271
110	0.15	240	0.221	370	0.275
120	0.156	250	0.226	380	0.278
130	0.163	260	0.23	390	0.282
				400	0.286

Your reaction time: .... Your partner's reaction time: ....

Analysis

3 Did your reaction time improve with practice? Suggest a reason for this.

....

....

4 Predict what your reaction time might be if the ruler was touching your hand when it was let go.

....

5 Plan and carry out a method to test your answer to Question 4.

....

....

....

....

Evaluation

6 Identify possible sources of error in the method and suggest improvements for these errors.

....

....

....

....

7 Suggest how you could change the method so that you test your reaction time with your hearing only.

....

....

Practical investigation 13.2 Sensitivity test

Objective

In this investigation, you will measure the sensitivity of different parts of your body and consider the reasons why some parts of the body are more sensitive than others.

Equipment

- Your body
- Piece of wire (or paper clip)

Method

1 Bend a piece of wire (or paper clip) so that the ends are 5 mm apart.
2 With your partner, discuss which parts of the body you will test for sensitivity.
3 Person A looks away or closes their eyes while person B touches the skin with the ends of the wire. Do not hit them or poke them with the wire; just press the wire firmly against the skin.
4 Person A states whether they can feel one or two points of the pin.
5 Test five different areas of the body, using the same amount of force, and record the results in the table below.
6 Person A and person B reverse roles and repeat steps 3–5. Check that the gap between the wires is 5 mm each time.

Safety considerations

- Do not press too hard with the wire.
- Do not press the wire on/in the eyes, mouth, inside the nose, ears or any other exposed area.

Recording data

1 Record your results in this table.

Area being tested	Points felt by student A	Points felt by student B

Analysis

2 State the areas that you could feel two points.

....

3 State the areas that you could feel only one point.

....

4 Suggest why you could feel two points in some areas but not in others.

....

....

Evaluation

5 For each test with the pins, you knew approximately where the pins would be placed. Outline how you could improve the method to make your data more reliable.

....

....

....

Practical investigation 13.3 Human responses

Objective

In this investigation, you will observe some involuntary responses of the human body in reaction to stimuli. You will link these responses to the use that the action has for the body.

Equipment

- Torch
- Half-metre ruler
- Chair
- Table or bench

Method

There are five different tests for you to do. Record your result or observation for each one in the table in the 'Recording data' section.

Test 1
1   Shine a torch briefly in your partner's eye. Record their reaction.

Test 2
2   Sit on the edge of a table or workbench. Sharply tap the point just below the knee with the ruler. Record the reaction of your partner.

Test 3
3   Wave your hand in front of your partner's face. Record their reaction.

Test 4
4   Remove your shoes and socks. Kneel on a chair so that your feet are hanging over the edge of the chair. Tap the back of the heel lightly with the ruler. Record your observation of the reaction.

Test 5
5   Draw a square on plain paper approximately $2\,cm^2$. Press lightly on the upper eyelid of one of your eyes for a few seconds. Release your eyelid and try to look at the box on the paper. Record the effect of this.

Safety considerations

- Take care when sitting and kneeling on the table and chair.
- Do not tap too hard when tapping the knee and the heel.
- Do not press too firmly on your eyelid.

Recording data

1   Record your observations in the following table.

Stimuli	Reaction
Shine torch in eye	
Tap below the knee	
Wave hand in front of eyes	
Tap back of heel	
Eyelid pressure and focus on box	

Analysis

2   Describe and explain the reaction to each of the stimuli in the table.

....

....

....

....

....

Evaluation

3   Suggest why some students in this investigation might have experienced different reactions.

....

....

Exam-style questions

1 Paddy investigates the response of a plant to light stimuli. He decides to grow a plant and observe its response to light stimuli. He places a maze box over a small bean plant. The box has a hole at the top for light to shine through, as shown in Figure 13.1.

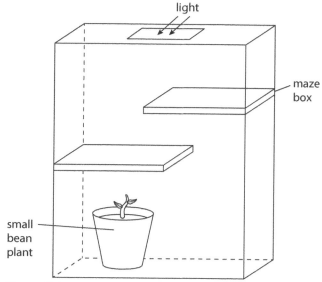

Figure 13.1

a On Figure 13.1, sketch the direction that the plant will grow over the next 5–6 days if watered and provided with nutrients. [2]

b State the name of the tropism that is evident in this investigation. [2]

....

c State the name of the plant hormone that promotes growth. [1]

....

d Define **negative phototropism**. [2]

....

....

Total [7]

2 **a** Identify the parts labelled X, Y and Z in Figure 13.2. [3]

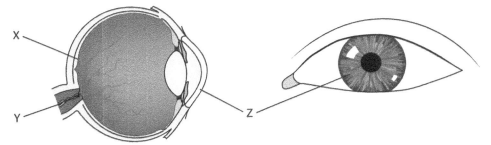

Figure 13.2

X ....

Y ....

Z ....

b Describe the function of part Y. [2]

....

....

c Outline what might happen if excessive light enters the eye onto part X. [2]

....

....

....

Total [7]

14 Homeostasis

Overview

In this chapter, you will investigate how the human body is affected by its external environment and how it responds in order to maintain a constant internal environment.

Practical investigation 14.1 Controlling body temperature

Objective

In this investigation, you will investigate how insulation affects the loss of heat energy from a controlled system. This will replicate how the body carries out thermoregulation to maintain its constant internal temperature.

Equipment

- Polystyrene cups × 4
- Different insulating materials
- Thermometer
- Elastic bands × 4
- Kettle or hot water source
- Stopwatch

Method

Plan your investigation with your partner/group and draw a suitable table for recording the data in the section below.

1   Select three of the insulation materials provided and cut them into the same size (by area), large enough to be able to surround the outside and top of the polystyrene cup.
2   Add hot water from the kettle to a polystyrene cup.
3   Immediately wrap one of the chosen materials around the cup, covering the top of the cup as well as the sides, securing in place with the elastic band.
4   Penetrate the material with the thermometer and record the starting temperature.
5   Start the stopwatch and leave the water for 5 minutes.
6   After 5 minutes, take the end temperature and record it in the table.
7   Repeat steps 2–6 for all of the materials, including one test without any material.

Safety considerations

Take care when handling hot water.

Recording data

1 Draw a table to record the starting temperature, the end temperature, the overall temperature change and the units for the different insulating materials that you investigated.

Handling data

2 Calculate the overall temperature change for each of the materials that you tested in the investigation. Record this in your table.

3 Calculate the percentage change in temperature for the material that had the greatest change in temperature. Show your working.

Answer: ....

Analysis

4 Describe the change in temperature for the insulating materials that you tested.

....

....

5 Explain how an insulating layer of material can reduce the loss of heat energy from a system.

....

....

6 The human body reacts to a drop in internal temperature by standing hairs on end to create an insulating layer of air above the skin. Outline how this investigation supports that this action is useful in thermoregulation.

....

....

....

Evaluation

7 Suggest why the insulating material had the same surface area.

....

....

8 Suggest how step 2 of the method could be changed to improve the validity of the investigation.

....

....

9 Outline why one test was carried out without using any material at all.

....

....

Practical investigation 14.2 Effect of body size on cooling rate

Objective

In this investigation, you will measure the effect of volume/size on the rate of cooling of water. You will link this to the effect of body size on the rate of cooling of the human body.

Equipment

- 50 ml glass beaker
- 100 ml glass beaker
- 250 ml glass beaker
- Thermometer
- Hot water
- Stopwatch

Method

1   Prepare a results table in the 'Recording data' section before you begin this investigation.
2   Pour the hot water into one of the beakers and fill to the halfway point.
3   Measure and record the temperature of the water and start the stopwatch. Take the temperature every minute for 10 minutes. The thermometer should be held so that it is halfway between the top of the water and the bottom of the beaker.
4   Repeat steps 2–3 for the other two beakers.

Safety considerations

Take care when handling hot water.

Recording data

1   Draw your results table in the following space.

Handling data

2 Plot a line graph for the change in temperature of each of the beakers over the 10-minute period.

Analysis

3 Using the line graph, outline how body size affects the rate of cooling of the body of water.

....

....

Evaluation

4 State the variables used in this investigation that were kept the same.

....

5 Explain why these variables were kept the same for the investigation.

....

....

Practical investigation 14.3 Evaporation rates from the skin

Objective

In this investigation, you will observe a simple investigation to measure the differing rates at which solutions evaporate. This reflects what happens as the evaporation of water removes heat energy from the skin in order to keep us cool.

Equipment

- Safety spectacles
- Thermometer × 3
- Test-tube rack or boss clamp × 3 and stand
- Cotton wool ball × 3
- Water
- Acetone

Method

1 Set up the three thermometers so that they are upside down. Do this in a test-tube rack or by using boss clamps and stands.
2 Prepare three cotton wool balls of equal size and wrap them around the bulb-end of the thermometer to create a large cotton swab.
3 Record the temperature of each thermometer.
4 Add enough water to soak the first cotton wool ball and record the change in temperature.
5 Repeat step 4, using the acetone and record the change in temperature. If using only one thermometer, you will need to allow the thermometer to return to the temperature of the surroundings.

Safety considerations

- Wear safety spectacles at all times.
- Wash hands after using acetone and do not ingest it.

Recording data

1 Prepare and complete a table to show the change in temperature of each of the cotton wool balls.

Analysis

2 Describe and explain the change in temperature of the three cotton wool balls.

....

....

3 If you spray perfume or aftershave onto your skin, it feels cold. Use the results from this investigation to explain why this happens.

....

....

4 Suggest how the removal of water in sweat from the skin by evaporation removes heat energy from the skin in order to keep you cool.

....

....

Evaluation

5 Draw a table in the space below to show how you would repeat the investigation to obtain data that are more reliable.

6 Suggest how the use of data loggers improves the investigation.

....

....

7 The third cotton wool ball was kept dry as a control. Suggest how this helped the investigation.

....

....

Exam-style questions

1 Define **homeostasis**. [1]

....

....

Total [1]

2 Ibrahim records his body temperature at 5-minute intervals for 30 minutes while standing in a cool room. He does not move during the investigation and records his temperature in a table, as shown:

Time/minutes	Temperature/°C
0	37.5
5	37.4
10	37.2
15	37.0
20	36.1
25	35.6
30	35.0

a Draw a suitable graph to show how Ibrahim's body temperature changed over time. [5]

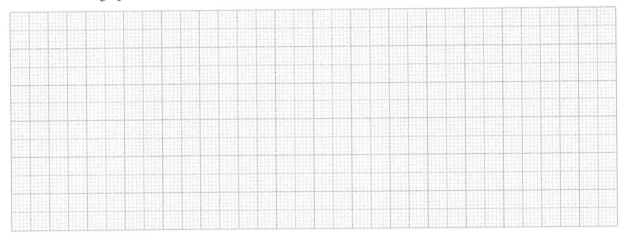

b Describe the change in body temperature for Ibrahim. [2]

....

....

c Outline what the thermoregulatory response of Ibrahim's body would be during the 30-minute period. [5]

....

....

....

....

....

Total [12]

15 Drugs

Overview

In this chapter, you will investigate the effect of caffeine on your reaction time and relate that to how chemical substances (drugs) can affect the human body. You will also investigate the effectiveness of different types of antibiotics, drugs used to tackle bacterial infections in animals including humans.

Practical investigation 15.1 Effect of caffeine on reaction times

Objective

In this investigation, you will repeat Practical investigation 13.1 completed earlier but this time with a new independent variable. You will investigate and observe the effect of caffeine on your reaction time and compare your data with that collected in Practical investigation 13.1.

Equipment

- Half-metre ruler
- Caffeinated drinks
- Stopwatch
- Table or bench to rest arm on

Method

1. Look back at your results from Practical investigation 13.1. Read the method and note your reaction time from that investigation.
2. Consume the caffeine drink and wait 15 minutes before beginning the test.
3. Use the 15-minute waiting time to plan the method that you will use to test the reaction times of you and your partner. You may refer to Practical investigation 13.1 to guide you.

....

....

....

....

....

Safety considerations

- Do not consume any other caffeine for the rest of the day.
- Do not drink more caffeine than guided by your teacher.
- You must have a signed note from your parent/guardian before beginning the investigation. Any student who does not have a note, or cannot drink caffeine, can still participate by working with their group to record results and ensure reliable testing.

Recording data

1 Note your reaction time from Practical investigation 13.1: ....
2 Prepare a table to record your results from this investigation.

Handling data

3 Use the reaction times convertor from Practical investigation 13.1 to calculate your reaction times from the distance that you caught the ruler.

Analysis

4 Describe the effect that caffeine had on your reaction time.

....

....

5 Explain the effect that caffeine had on your reaction time.

....

....

....

Evaluation

6 Suggest why there was a 15-minute period between drinking the caffeine and testing the reaction times.

....

....

7 A blind test would mean that some students would consume caffeine and some students would not drink caffeine. The students would not know whether they had consumed caffeine until after completion of the test.

   a Outline how you would plan a blind experiment for this investigation, using a caffeinated drink and a decaffeinated drink.

....

....

....

....

   b Suggest why a blind test might be used.

....

....

8 Outline any ethical issues with testing the effect of caffeine on students.

....

....

....

Practical investigation 15.2 Effect of antibiotics on bacteria

Objective

In this investigation, you will observe how three different antibiotics affect a bacterial culture under ideal conditions. This will support your understanding of how the body can be protected from bacterial infection.

Equipment

- Safety spectacles
- Disinfectant
- Sterile agar plate (Petri dish)
- Marker pen
- Incubator
- Microbe sample in nutrient broth
- Antibiotic discs × 3
- Bunsen burner and heat mat
- Inoculating loop
- Sticky tape

Method

1. Wash your hands with soap and water and clean your workbench with the disinfectant.
2. Label the sterile agar plate with your name.
3. Turn on your Bunsen burner and use the hotter flame for the next steps.
4. Heat the inoculating loop until it is glowing red-hot.
5. Unscrew the bottle of nutrient broth containing the microbe sample and hold the opening of the bottle in the flame for 2–3 seconds.
6. Turn off the Bunsen burner.
7. Place the loop into the microbe sample and replace the lid on the bottle.
8. Lift the lid of the Petri dish so that you can just fit the inoculating loop inside. Gently move the loop over the surface of the agar and replace the lid.
9. Place the antibiotic discs onto the agar plate. Sketch a diagram to record where each disc (use the code and key provided by the teacher) is located on the agar.
10. Seal the Petri dish with the sticky tape.
11. Place the dish upside down in the incubator at 25 °C for 2 days (or your next lesson if this is the next day or after the weekend).
12. Wash your hands with soap and water and clean your workbench with the disinfectant.
13. **DO NOT OPEN THE SEALED PETRI DISH AT ANY POINT.**
14. When you get your Petri dish back, observe what has happened inside. Make a labelled drawing of what you see in the 'Recording data' section.

Safety considerations

- Wear safety spectacles at all times.
- Clean all equipment with disinfectant or similar solution, before and after the investigation.
- Do not open the sealed Petri dish.
- Take care when setting up and using the Bunsen burner.
- Do not eat or drink in the laboratory.
- Do not ingest or inhale the contents of the Petri dish or the bottle of nutrient broth.
- Cover all open wounds or cuts.

Recording data

1 State the name of the antibiotics that you used

- Disc X ....

- Disc Y ....

- Disc Z ....

2 Draw and label what happened in your Petri dish after 48 hours in the incubator.

Handling data

3 Without opening the dish, measure the diameter of the clear zone around each disc.

a Disc X ....

b Disc Y ....

c Disc Z ....

Analysis

4 State the name of the disc that had the largest diameter of the clear zone.

....

5 Suggest why this disc had the largest diameter for the clear zone.

....

....

Evaluation

6 Suggest what might happen if the strict safety rules were not followed in this investigation.

....

....

Exam-style questions

1 Figure 15.1 shows the results of an investigation carried out by Lynne. Lynne placed three discs, X, Y and Z, onto an agar plate containing a known bacterium. Two of the discs had been soaked in different antibiotics and one disc had been soaked in water as a control.

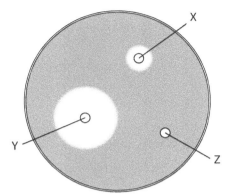

Figure 15.1

a State which antibiotic had the greatest effect on the bacteria. [1]

....

b Describe the effect of the two antibiotics on the bacteria in the investigation. [2]

....

....

c State which disc was soaked in water as the control to the experiment. [1]

....

d Explain how you know which disc was soaked in water. [1]

....

....

e Suggest a reason for using a control in this investigation. [1]

....

....

Total [6]

2 Describe and explain the effect of smoking tobacco on the cells in the trachea. [5]

....

....

....

....

....

Total [5]

3 Some of the particles contained in tobacco tar are carcinogens. Define **carcinogen**. [1]

....

....

Total [1]

16 Reproduction in plants

Overview

In this chapter, you will investigate the structure of a flowering plant and describe some of the parts that you can see. You will investigate the requirements for successful germination of cress seeds and explore the temperature dependence of plant growth. The close link between plant reproduction and the conditions required for germination is reviewed in this chapter.

Practical investigation 16.1 Structure of a flower

Objective

In this investigation, you will observe, measure and record the structure of a flower from an insect-pollinated flowering plant.

Equipment

- Scalpel
- Hand lens
- Flower
- Microscope slide
- Microscope

Method

1   Remove the sepals and the petals of the flower by pulling them downwards in the direction of the stem. Do not discard any of the parts of the flower that you remove.
2   Use the hand lens to examine one of the petals and make a large labelled drawing of the petal in the 'Recording data' section below.
3   Remove the stamens by cutting them carefully with the scalpel. Transfer the pollen grains onto a microscope slide and observe them under the microscope. Make a large labelled drawing of a pollen grain in the 'Recording data' section.
4   Remove all parts of the flower until just the carpel remains. Make a longitudinal cut to reveal the hollow insides of the carpel. Make a large labelled diagram of the inside of the carpel in the 'Recording data' section.
5   Your teacher may provide you with two different plants. If so, repeat steps 1–4 for the second plant and compare the similarities and differences between the two plants.

Safety considerations

Take care when handling the scalpel.

Recording data

1   Make your labelled drawings in the spaces below.

Drawing of a petal

Drawing of a pollen grain

Drawing of the inside of a carpel

Analysis

2 For your drawing of the petal, calculate the magnification of your drawing compared to the actual petal. Show your working.

....

....

3 Take the parts of the flower that you removed or dissected and stick them to a blank piece of A4 paper. Label each part and outline the function of each part that you removed. Your flower posters will make a valuable classroom resource.

Practical investigation 16.2 Oxygen for germination

Objective

In this investigation, you will observe a demonstration by your teacher. You will make predictions about what will happen and comment on the results produced. You will observe the importance of oxygen for germination. Germination of seeds occurs after fertilisation of plants and so the environmental conditions for plants have an important role to play in plant reproduction.

Equipment

- Alkaline pyrogallol
- Water
- Boiling tube ×2
- Sewing thread to suspend the cotton wool
- Bung for boiling tube ×2
- Cress seeds on moist cotton wool ×2
- Safety spectacles

Method

This is a teacher demonstration for safety reasons but the method is outlined here for your observation and use.

1   Set up two boiling tubes, A and B, as shown in Figure 16.1.

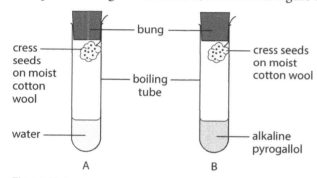

Figure 16.1

2   Alkaline pryogallol absorbs oxygen. Use this information to make a prediction for what will happen in boiling tube A and B in the 'Recording data' section.
3   Leave the two boiling tubes in a safe place for 48 hours and observe.
4   Record the differences and compare them to your predictions.

Safety considerations

- Wear safety spectacles at all times.
- Alkaline pryogallol is a caustic substance and must be handled *only* by a teacher who has observed the relevant safety precautions for use.
- Do not eat or drink in the laboratory.

Recording data

1   Make your predictions for what will happen in each of the boiling tubes:
   a Boiling tube A:

   ....

   ....

b Boiling tube B:

....

....

After 48 hours, note your observations for each boiling tube:

c Boiling tube A:

....

....

d Boiling tube B:

....

....

Analysis

2 Describe the differences between the contents of the two boiling tubes.

....

....

3 Alkaline pryogallol absorbs oxygen. Describe and explain the effect that this had on the cress seeds.

....

....

Evaluation

4 Outline why boiling tube A contained water.

....

....

5 Alkaline pryogallol is a caustic substance. State why this investigation had to be carried out by the teacher.

....

....

6 Predict what would happen if the seeds from boiling tube B were removed and placed into boiling tube A for 48 hours.

....

....

Practical investigation 16.3 Measuring the effect of temperature on the germination of cress seeds

Objective

In this investigation, you will investigate and observe the effect of temperature on the germination of cress seeds. You will plan your own investigation using the information provided. Germination of seeds occurs after fertilisation of plants and so the environmental conditions for plants have an important role to play in plant reproduction.

Equipment

- Cress seeds × 15
- Petri dish
- Cotton wool or paper towels
- Access to a refrigerator

Method

Cress seeds require the following conditions for germination:
- Damp cotton wool or paper towel placed inside a Petri dish
- Keep the seeds in a damp, but not soaked, condition
- Seedlings will take up to 10–14 days for maximum growth without extra nutrients being provided but you can compare the rate of germination in each lesson during that time.

1 Use this information to plan a method to germinate cress seeds in three different temperatures and to record the rates of germination of the resulting cress seedlings over a period of 14 days.

....
....
....
....
....
....

Safety considerations

Wash your hands after handling the seeds.

Recording data

2 Prepare a results table to record the heights of the cress seedlings over the course of your investigation. Include a column in your table to calculate the number of seeds that germinated.

Handling data

3 Calculate the number of seeds that germinated in each of the different temperatures. Use germination (%) = no. of seeds that germinated/no. of seeds in tray × 100.

    a Number of seeds, temperature A: ....

    b Number of seeds, temperature B: ....

    c Number of seeds, temperature C: ....

Total [9]

Analysis

4 Describe and explain the results of your investigation.

....

....

....

....

Exam-style questions

1

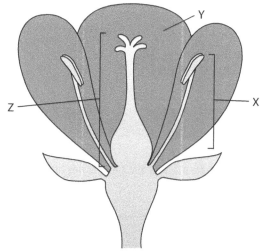

Figure 16.2

a State the name of the part of the flower labelled X in Figure 16.2. [1]

....

b Describe the function of the part of the flower labelled X. [2]

....

....

c State the name of the part of the flower labelled Z. [1]

....

d Describe the function of the part of the flower labelled Z. [2]

....

....

e Make a large labelled drawing of the part of the flower labelled Y. [5]

Total [11]

17 Reproduction in humans

Overview

In this chapter, you will model how the human body prepares for giving birth to ensure that the fetus is not damaged by external forces.

Practical investigation 17.1 Protecting the fetus

Objective

In this investigation, you will model how the amniotic fluid in the uterus protects the growing fetus. It is not practical to carry out investigations in this unit but, like all scientists, it is important that you are still able to observe parts of the unit in action. Although you will be using chicken eggs, this section will **model** how the fetus is protected in humans.

Equipment

- Eggs × 2
- Metre stick or tape measure
- Sealable plastic bags × 2
- Newspapers

Method

1 Place an egg into each of the bags.
2 Fill one of the bags to the top with water and seal both bags securely.
3 Prepare the area for testing – this area needs to be clear of personal belongings, books and electrical equipment.
4 Drop the bag that contains the egg and no water from a height of 1 m.
5 Observe and record what happens to the egg.
6 Repeat steps 4–5 with the bag that contains the water and the egg.

Safety considerations

- Clear all belongings from the testing area and line with newspapers.
- Be aware of any spillages on the floor.

Recording data

1 Outline what happened to each of the eggs in the investigation.

....
....
....
....

Analysis

2 State which part of the female reproductive system is represented by the water.

....

3 State which part of the reproductive process is represented by the eggs.

....

4 Describe how the answer to Question 2 protects the feature named in Question 3.

....
....
....

Evaluation

5 Suggest why an egg was dropped without water.

....
....

Exam-style questions

1 Figure 17.1 shows the concentration of different hormones during a 28-day cycle of a female human.

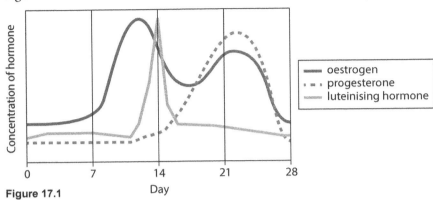

Figure 17.1

a State the name of the gland that luteinising hormone is produced by. [1]

....

b State what happens because of the increase in concentration of luteinising hormone on day 14. [1]

....

c State the name of the hormones in Figure 17.1 produced in the ovaries. [2]

....

d The concentration of progesterone decreases shortly after day 21. Explain why this decrease happens. [3]

....

....

e Suggest and explain what would happen to the concentration of progesterone after day 21 if the female became pregnant. [3]

....

....

....

Total [10]

2 Figure 17.2 shows a human fetus during pregnancy.

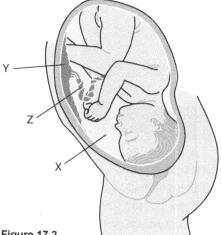

Figure 17.2

a State the name of the structure labelled X. [1]

....

b Describe the function of X. [2]

....

....

c Suggest why Figure 17.2 shows a fetus and not an embryo. [2]

....

....

d State the name of substances that may be exchanged at the part named Y. [3]

....

....

....

Total [8]

18 Inheritance

Overview

In order to observe inheritance, it is necessary to observe what happens to different generations as genetic variation takes place from one generation to the next. Unless you remain at school for hundreds of years, this is not possible to investigate in your own laboratory. Scientists often use animals such as *Xenopus laevis* (African clawed frog) as these have a much shorter life cycle and genetic changes and development can be observed easily. As you do not have access to lots of African clawed frogs, this unit will look at how asexual reproduction produces clones. You should apply your knowledge of sexual reproduction from the remainder of the unit to fully understand how genetic variation takes place in sexual reproduction. You will also use your knowledge of inheritance to predict, and observe, the ratios of producing offspring with a particular characteristic.

Practical investigation 18.1 Cloning a cauliflower

Objective

In this investigation, you will use your knowledge of asexual reproduction to clone a piece of cauliflower in less than 2 weeks. You will compare the cloned cauliflower to that of its parent.

Equipment

- Floret of cauliflower
- Forceps
- Scalpel
- Disinfectant solution
- 50 ml glass beaker
- Stopwatch

- Distilled water (sterile)
- 250 ml glass beaker × 2
- Petri dish × 2
- Bunsen burner
- Test-tube containing agar growth medium × 2

- Aluminium foil
- Marker pen
- Safety spectacles
- Disposable gloves
- Aprons/lab coats

Method

This is a lengthy method to avoid contamination of the florets and must be followed carefully. Read the safety considerations **before** starting.

1 Wipe down the work surfaces with disinfectant.
2 Cut off a small piece of cauliflower floret with the scalpel. The piece of cauliflower should be no longer than 5 mm in any direction.
3 Cut the cauliflower into two small pieces. These pieces are known as explants and should be placed into the 50 ml glass beaker that contains the disinfectant solution. Leave the explants in the disinfectant for 15 minutes, giving the beaker a gentle swirl every 2 minutes.

4   Fill the two 250 ml beakers with 100 ml of the sterile distilled water and cover to avoid contamination. Use the Petri dishes or similar apparatus for this.

5   Turn on the Bunsen burner and place the forceps into the Bunsen burner and leave to cool.

6   When the 15 minutes has passed, transfer the explants into the first beaker of distilled water, and leave for 1 minute.

7   During this minute, sterilise the forceps in the Bunsen flame and leave to cool.

8   Transfer the explants into the second beaker of distilled water and leave for 1 minute.

9   During this minute, sterilise the forceps again and flame the end of the first test-tube that contains the agar growth medium.

10 Place one of the explants into the test-tube with the cool, flamed forceps and cover tightly with aluminium foil. Do this quickly to minimise contamination.

11 Place the second explant into the flamed, test-tube with the cool, flamed forceps and cover tightly with aluminium foil. Do this quickly to minimise contamination.

12 Label the test-tubes with the marker pen.

13 Wipe down the work surfaces with disinfectant.

14 Leave the tubes in a warm, well-lit location and observe after 2 weeks.

15 Observe and record your results.

Safety considerations

- Wear safety spectacles at all times.
- Wear gloves when handling the disinfectant and wash hands afterwards.
- Wear protective apron or lab coat.
- Take care using the Bunsen burner and beware of the hot forceps after flaming.
- Take care when using the scalpel.
- Contamination leads to growth of fungi and bacteria. Your teacher will observe the growth of the cauliflower to ensure that harmful pathogens do not grow.

Recording data

1   Outline your observations in the following spaces:

   a After 1 week:

   ....

   ....

   b After 2 weeks:

   ....

   ....

Analysis

2   **a** If the new pieces of cauliflower floret that have grown were genetically compared to the original explants, suggest how their DNA would compare.

   ....

b Explain your answer to part a.

....

....

Evaluation

3 Outline why this method has so many steps to avoid contamination of the explants and the equipment used.

....

....

Exam-style question

1 Jack breeds cats for a living. He breeds a cat with black fur with a cat that has brown fur.

a The colour of the fur is an example of one of the cats' phenotypes. Define **phenotype**. [1]

....

....

b The cat with black fur is homozygous for black fur. Define **homozygous**. [2]

....

....

c The cat with the brown fur is homozygous for brown fur. The allele for black fur is dominant and the allele for the brown fur is recessive.

  i Define **allele**. [1]

....

  ii Define **dominant**. [1]

....

  iii Define **recessive**. [1]

....

....

d Use a genetic diagram to predict the likelihood of producing offspring with brown fur. [3]

Answer: ....

e State the likelihood of producing offspring with black fur. [1]

....

Total [10]

19 Variation and natural selection

Overview

In this chapter, you will investigate how humans exhibit variation and the reasons behind this. You will investigate the adaptive features of a leaf that help those organisms to survive in their environment.

Practical investigation 19.1 Variation in humans

Objective

In this investigation, you will investigate different inherited characteristics within your class and use the data to suggest patterns and similarities.

Equipment

- Tape measure/metre stick
- Graph paper (1 cm²)
- Pencil

Method

1 You are going to survey the following features of at least 10 of your classmates.
   a Height (m) – use the tape measure/metre stick
   b Arm span (m) – use the tape measure
   c Hand size (cm²) – using the graph paper, draw around the hand and calculate the total area
   d Eye colour
   e Hair colour
2 Prepare a table in the 'Recording data' section.
3 Complete your table by surveying your classmates.

Safety considerations

Take care when moving around the room.

Recording data

1 Prepare your table in the space provided.

Handling data

2 Look at the data collected in your table.

a Divide the data gathered for hand size into five suitable categories. For example, 80–100 cm², 100–120 cm², etc. Tally the number of students that fit into each category.

Hand size / cm²	Number of students

b Draw a histogram to show the results for hand size of the people in your class.

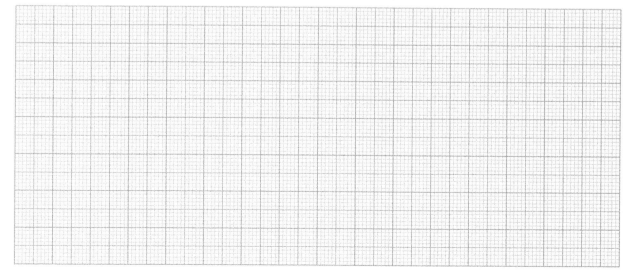

3 Plot a bar chart to show the number of students with each eye colour.

Analysis

4 Describe the pattern of variation for hand size in your class.

....

....

5 State whether the data for hand size is continuous or discontinuous variation.

....

6 State any characteristics which may be inherited in this investigation.

....

....

Evaluation

7 Outline how you could improve the reliability of the data that you have collected.

....

....

Practical investigation 19.2 Adaptive features

Objective

In this investigation, you will investigate and observe one of the main adaptive features of a leaf that helps plants to survive in their environment.

Equipment

- Leaf from a plant kept in sunlight
- Leaf from a plant kept in darkness
- Clear nail varnish
- Microscope slide
- Light microscope
- Transparent cellophane tape

Method

1. Label each of the leaves for identity later. Add a thick layer of the clear nail varnish to the underside of one of the leaves.
2. Allow the nail varnish to dry completely. This can take several minutes for some varnishes.
3. Once the varnish is hard and dry, place a piece of the cellophane tape over the varnished area and gently peel it back. This will lift the varnish from the leaf, which now contains an imprint of the underside of the leaf.
4. Place your varnish sample onto the microscope slide and trim away any excess tape.
5. Observe under the light microscope at a magnification of × 400. Locate an area with several stomata in clear view.
6. Make a labelled drawing of what you see in the 'Recording data' section.
7. Repeat steps 1–6 for the second leaf.

Safety considerations

Wash hands if skin in contact with nail varnish.

Recording data

Make a labelled drawing of what you can see in the field of view for each of the two leaves.

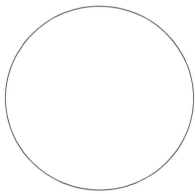

leaf in sunlight

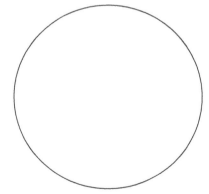

leaf in darkness

Handling data

1 Count the number of open stomata in each of the samples.

   a Leaf in sunlight: ....

   b Leaf in darkness: ....

Analysis

2 Describe and explain the difference between the numbers of open stomata that you observed.

   ....

   ....

   ....

Evaluation

3 Suggest why it is important to use leaves from the same species of plant in this investigation.

   ....

   ....

4 Suggest how the comparison of open stomata in darkness and in light could be made more reliable in this investigation.

   ....

   ....

Exam-style question

1 Mr Amoroso is carrying out a survey to gather data about the mass of the students who attend his classes. He surveys 71 students and records their mass in categories in the following table.

Mass / kg	Number of boys	Number of girls
30–40	1	3
41–50	7	9
51–60	16	15
61–70	5	6
71–80	4	2
81+	2	1

   a State the type of variation that Mr Amoroso has measured. [1]

   ....

b Draw a suitable graph/chart to show the data collected by Mr Amoroso. [4]

c Describe the pattern of data collected by Mr Amoroso. [2]

....

....

d Suggest one reason why the data for the mass of the students can be considered reliable. [1]

....

Total [8]

20 Organisms and their environment

Overview

In this chapter, you will investigate how organisms interact with their environment and how population sizes may affect the biotic factors around them.

Practical investigation 20.1 Using a quadrat

Objective

In this investigation, you will investigate and observe population sizes for a chosen organism in your local area. You will use the data gathered to describe the biodiversity of the area.

Equipment

- Quadrat
- Smartphone or digital camera

Method

1 Observe the area that you are going to survey. You will need to select how many times you will place your quadrat and where you will place it.
2 For each quadrat, count the number of each species that is present in that area. If you do not know the name of a species, take a photograph of it, make a note of it in your table in the 'Recording data' section, and use this to research the species name later.
3 Note the environmental conditions of each quadrat – level of light, shade, access to water, predators or animals present.
4 Repeat the quadrat sample as directed by your teacher. It is better to collect as much data from as many different areas as possible.

Safety considerations

- Do not handle any organisms with your hands.
- Do not remove any organisms from their natural habitat.
- Do not throw the quadrat in the direction of other students.

Recording data

1 Prepare a table in the following space to record the population sizes for each quadrat sample taken.

Handling data

2 Draw a bar chart to show the relative population sizes for the species counted in the area surveyed.

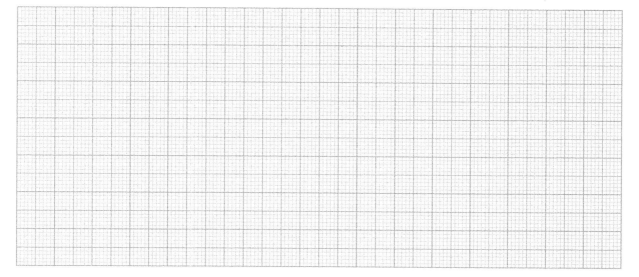

Analysis

3 Describe the data that you have collected from this investigation.

....

....

....

4 Discuss how the population size varies from one area to another.

....

....

....

5 Suggest why some areas had larger populations of the same species than others.

....

....

Evaluation

6 Explain why more than one quadrat sample was taken.

....

....

7 Suggest why you did not count every single organism for the area covered in the investigation.

....

....

8 Explain why the quadrat was placed in random locations during the interview during the investigation.

....

....

Practical investigation 20.2 Making compost

Objective

In this investigation, you will make your own compost column and use this to confirm which materials will or will not decompose.

Equipment

- 2-litre plastic bottle
- 1 kg soil
- Kitchen waste
- Scalpel or knife

- Organic waste
- Mounted needle
- Bunsen burner
- Water

- Pipette
- Aluminium foil
- Elastic band
- Non-biodegradable waste

Method

1 Use the scalpel, knife or scissors to cut off the top of the plastic bottle at the point where the label begins (remove the label).
2 Fill the bottom third of the bottle with soil.
3 Add a loose layer of organic waste and a loose layer of soil.
4 Add a loose layer of kitchen waste and a loose layer of soil.
5 Add a loose layer of non-biodegradable waste and a loose layer of soil.
6 Pipette some water to each layer of the soil for steps 3–5; just enough to add moisture to each layer.
7 Turn on the Bunsen burner and heat the end of the mounted needle.
8 When the needle is red-hot, use the needle to pierce several small holes on the side of the bottle. The holes must be small enough to avoid the soil spilling out.
9 Cover the top of the bottle with the foil and secure with the elastic band. Pierce a few holes in the foil.
10 Shake the bottles every few days to circulate air.
11 Observe the bottles after 4, 8 and 12 weeks. This is a long investigation but will be a useful recap when you have to think back to what you did!

Safety considerations

- Take care when using the scalpel or sharp knife.
- Cover any jagged edges of plastic with insulation tape to avoid cuts.
- Wash hands after handling waste or soil.
- Do not add dairy or meat products as these will smell.

Recording data

1   Record your observations below.
Date compost made: ....
4-week date and observation:

....

....

8-week date and observation:

....

....

12-week date and observation:

....

....

Analysis

2   Describe the difference between the rates of decomposition for the three different types of waste in your compost column.

....

....

3   It is possible to test for nitrates with nitrate strips. State the layer of your compost that would most likely test positive for nitrates or nitrites.

....

4   State the name of the chemical reaction that breaks down plant and animal protein to ammonium ions.

....

Evaluation

5   Suggest how the addition of worms to your compost would affect the rate of decomposition for your waste products.

....

....

Exam-style question

1   Figure 20.1 shows the changes for a population of bacteria.

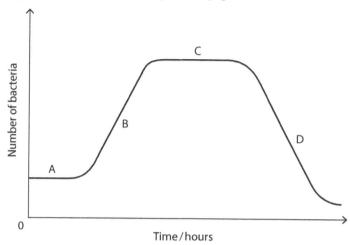

Figure 20.1

a State the name of the phase in part A of the curve [1]. ....

b State the name of the phase in part B of the curve [1]. ....

c State the name of the phase in part C of the curve [1]. ....

d State the name of the phase in part D of the curve [1]. ....

e Explain why the rate of growth increases in part B of the curve [2].

....

....

f Suggest why the population decreases in part D of the curve [2].

....

....

Total [8]

21 Biotechnology

Overview

In this chapter, you will investigate how bacteria are used in biotechnology and in the production of food and drink. You will observe and investigate the use of pectinase in industry and at home.

Practical investigation 21.1 Effect of pectinase on apple pulp

Objective

In this investigation, you will observe the effect of the enzyme pectinase on apple pulp.

Equipment

- 100 g of apple
- 250 ml glass beaker × 2
- 100 cm³ measuring cylinder × 2
- Glass stirring rod × 2
- Stopwatch

- Balance
- Pectinase
- Safety spectacles
- Water bath or incubator, 40 °C
- Knife

- Chopping board
- Clingfilm
- Funnel × 2
- Filter paper × 2

Method

1 Chop the apple into small pieces. These should be no larger than 5 mm³.
2 Divide the 100 g of apple into two separate beakers.
3 Add 2 ml of pectinase to one of the beakers and stir with the glass rod.
4 Add 2 ml of water to the second beaker of apple and stir with the glass rod.
5 Cover the beakers with Clingfilm and incubate at 40 °C for 20 minutes.
6 Line the funnels with the filter paper.
7 Place the funnel over the measuring cylinder and add the pulp from each beaker.
8 Record the volume of juice obtained from each sample of apple pulp every 5 minutes until the juice no longer filters through the paper.

Safety considerations

- Wear safety spectacles.
- Take care when using the scalpel or knife.
- Handle pectinase with care. Wash hands after use or if contact is made with the pectinase.
- Immediately clean up any spillages.

Recording data

1 Record your data in the table.

Apple	Volume of juice produced/ml							
	0 min	5 min	10 min	15 min	20 min	25 min	30 min	35 min
with pectinase								
in water								

Handling data

2 Draw a line graph to show the amount of apple juice produced over time.

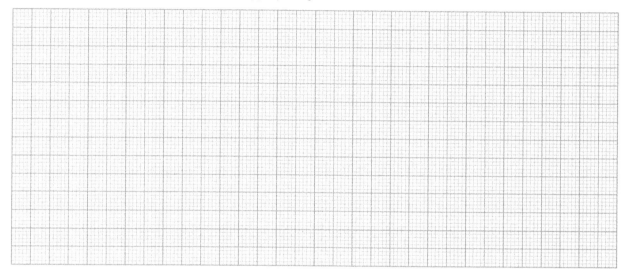

Analysis

3 Describe the effect of pectinase on the amount of juice produced from apple pulp.

....

....

4 Explain why the pectinase had this effect on the production of apple juice from pulp.

....

....

....

Evaluation

5 Suggest why the investigation was carried out using water.

....

....

Practical investigation 21.2 Effect of temperature on pectinase

Objective

In this investigation, you will plan your own investigation to see what temperature pectinase will work most effectively at. This will be measured by the amount of juice produced from a sample of apple pulp.

Equipment

- 100 g of apple
- 250 ml glass beakers
- 100 cm³ measuring cylinders
- Glass stirring rods
- Stopwatch
- Balance
- Pectinase
- Safety spectacles
- Water bath or incubator
- Knife
- Chopping board
- Clingfilm
- Funnels
- Filter paper

Method

1   Your task is to plan a method that will allow you to compare the effect of pectinase at three different temperatures. Plan your method below.

....

....

....

....

....

....

....

....

....

....

2   State the three different temperatures at which you will test the effect of pectinase on apple pulp.

   a   ....°C

   b   ....°C

   c   ....°C

Safety considerations

- Wash your hands after handling pectinase.

3   State two other safety precautions that you must take.

....

....

Recording data

4 Prepare a table to record the total amount of juice produced from apple pulp at the three different temperatures selected.

Analysis

5 State the temperature at which pectinase worked best on the apple pulp.

....

6 Suggest how you know that this is the temperature that pectinase worked at.

....

....

7 Use your knowledge of enzymes to suggest why the pectinase worked best at this temperature.

....

....

....

8 Outline how this knowledge of pectinase is useful in commercial juice production.

....

....

Evaluation

9 Outline how the reliability and validity of the investigation could be improved.

....

....

Practical investigation 21.3 Biological washing powders

Objective

In this investigation, you will investigate the effect of different washing powders on removing egg stains from a piece of material.

Equipment

- Piece of white material × 2
- Egg
- Paper towels
- Spoon
- Plastic tray
- 250 ml glass beaker × 2
- 100 ml glass beaker
- Stirring rod
- Kettle
- Biological washing powder
- Non-biological washing powder
- Stopwatch

Method

1   Break the egg into the 100 ml glass beaker.
2   Stir the egg to break the yolk and mix the contents.
3   Over the plastic tray, spoon some of the egg mixture onto the white material. Use your hands to rub the egg into the material. Use the paper towel to absorb any excess egg.
4   Leave the material to dry; this will be much faster in a warm place, such as in direct sunlight or by a heat source.
5   In the meantime, prepare the beakers and label accordingly. Add 200 ml of warm water from the kettle (as close to 40–50 °C as possible) to each of the 250 ml glass beakers.
6   Add two spoonfuls of the biological washing powder to one of the beakers, and two spoonfuls of the non-biological washing powder to the second beaker.
7   Add the two pieces of stained material to the beakers at the same time, check that they are both at the same temperature, and begin the stopwatch.
8   Leave the material in the water for 15 minutes before removing and drying near a heat source, such as a radiator or in direct sunlight.
9   Observe the difference in stains and record your observations in the 'Recording data' section.

Safety considerations

- Wash hands after handling the washing powders and egg.
- Clean the work surfaces with disinfectant.

Recording data

1 Sketch and label the difference between the two pieces of material in the boxes below.

[box]

biological washing powder

[box]

non-biological washing powder

Analysis

2 Describe the difference in the stains after being soaked in the washing powder solutions.

....

....

3 Suggest the reasons for your results.

....

....

4 Eggs contain protein. Suggest the name of an enzyme that would be suitable for breaking down the egg stains.

....

Evaluation

5 Outline how you could investigate the effect of the biological washing powder at different temperatures.

....

....

....

....

....

Exam-style question

1   Pectinase, protease and lipase are useful enzymes in industry and at home.

   a Describe and explain how these enzymes are used in the home or in industry. [6]

   ....
   ....
   ....
   ....
   ....
   ....
   ....
   ....

   b Outline a method to test the effect of pH on the activity of pectinase. [5]

   ....
   ....
   ....
   ....
   ....
   ....

   Total [11]

22 Humans and the environment

Overview

In this chapter, you will investigate how humans have affected the environment and how this can be measured. You will use this information to make assumptions about what has caused the changes and what needs to happen in order to prevent further damage.

Practical investigation 22.1 Effect of acid on the germination of cress seeds

Objective

In this investigation, you will investigate and observe the effect that acid 'rain' has on the germination of cress seeds.

Equipment

- Safety spectacles
- Cress seeds
- Different strength acids
- Pipettes
- Paper towels
- Petri dishes
- Water

Method

1   Select three acids at different concentrations for this investigation. Record the concentrations in the table in the 'Recording data' section.
2   Prepare four Petri dishes with a paper towel in the bottom of each dish.
3   Place eight cress seeds into each of the Petri dishes.
4   Soak the paper towel in each of the labelled Petri dishes using the correct acid solution or distilled water.
5   Observe what happens over the next 7 days and record your observations in the table.

Safety considerations

- Wear safety spectacles at all times.
- Wash hands if in contact with irritant acids.

Recording data

1 Record the different concentrations of your acid solutions and your observations in the table.

Cress seeds 'watered' with:	Observation after 1 week
distilled water	
acid .... M	
acid .... M	
acid .... M	

Analysis

2 Describe and explain the effect the different acid solutions had on the germination rate of the cress seeds.

....

....

3 Suggest how the investigation shows the effect that humans can have on the environment.

....

....

....

Evaluation

4 Outline how the investigation could be improved to produce data that compares the growth rate of the cress seedlings.

....

....

....

Practical investigation 22.2 Fossil fuel combustion

Objective

In this investigation, you will investigate and observe what happens when coal is heated. You will link this to the human impact on the environment.

Equipment

- Small lumps of coal
- Bunsen burner
- Boss clamp and stand
- Cotton wool
- Heat mat
- Double delivery tube system (see diagram)
- Universal Indicator
- Conical flask
- Vacuum pump or fume cupboard
- Safety spectacles

Method

1 Set up the equipment as shown in Figure 22.1.
2 Turn on the Bunsen burner and begin to heat the coal.
3 Observe what happens to the cotton wool and the Universal Indicator.
4 Sketch a diagram of what happens in the 'Recording data' section.

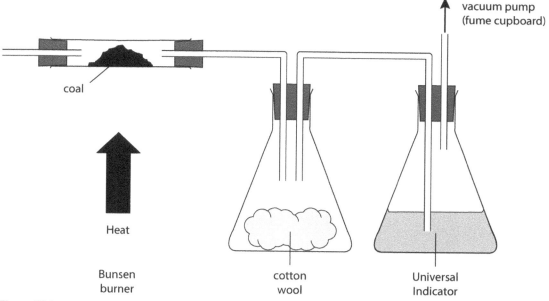

Figure 22.1

Safety considerations

- Wear safety spectacles at all times.
- Carry out the investigation in a fume cupboard (your teacher will demonstrate this) or by using a vacuum pump to collect the gases formed by the combustion of the coal.
- Take care when using the hot Bunsen burner and do not handle the equipment until it has cooled.

Recording data

1 Sketch a diagram to show what happened to the cotton wool and the Universal Indicator in the investigation.

Analysis

2 Describe the effect that burning coal had on:

a The cotton wool

....

b The Universal Indicator

....

3 Suggest how the change in colour of the Universal Indicator supports your understanding of how acid rain is formed.

....

....

4 Predict and explain what would happen if the investigation was repeated using limewater in place of the Universal Indicator.

....

....

Evaluation

5 Outline how you could investigate the effect of burning different quantities of coal on the acidity of the gases produced.

....

....

....

....

....

Exam-style question

1 Discuss the causes and effects of acid rain. [6]

....

....

....

....

....

....

....

....

....

....

Total [6]